WHILE 70% OF all organizational change initiatives fail, this one succeeded – and improved telecom producer Mitel Corporation's bottom line profitability by a factor of 40.

Like many organizations, Mitel's entrenched processes, procedures and policies – its "Sacred Cows" – had resulted in products that were slow getting to market. When they did get to market many products had quality problems. The sluggish company culture was also making it impossible for Mitel to face a looming technology shift and do battle with new brand of competitors who threatened to wipe the company out.

Authors Geoff Smith and Stephen Quesnelle were front and center driving the change that saved Mitel: Geoff as the Vice President of Research and Development with 500 engineers reporting to him and Stephen as the Organizational Development (OD) professional partnered with Geoff to help lead the turnaround.

Refreshing and engaging, this book tells how Geoff and Stephen met the challenge head-on. They used a behavior based leadership approach based on over 50 years of scientific research, plus their own creative initiatives to "kill" the Sacred Cows.

More than a fascinating case study, this book provides all the hard-hitting lessons learned by the company, by Geoff as the Change Champion and by Stephen as the Change Agent. *In the Company of Sacred Cows* provides you with a framework for making organizational change in your company. Whether your business is growing or shrinking, this book provides you with a how-to manual with the real-life tools and techniques you need to meet rapidly changing business demands.

In The Company of Sacred Cows

A True Story of Organizational Change

AuthorHouse™
1663 Liberty Drive, Suite 200
Bloomington, IN 47403
www.authorhouse.com
Phone: 1-800-839-8640

All rights reserved under International and Pan-American Copyright Conventions. No part of this publication may be stored in a database or retrieval system or reproduced, distributed, or transmitted in any form by any means, including photocopying, scanning, recording, or other mechanical or electronic methods, without the prior written permission of the publishers, except in the case of brief quotations embodied in critical reviews and certain other non-commercial uses permitted by copyright law. For permission requests, contact Sacred Cow Company, www.sacredcowcompany.com

© *2009 Stephen Quesnelle and Geoff Smith. All rights reserved.*

Grateful acknowledgement is made to Universal Press Syndicate for permission to reprint Calvin & Hobbes. Copyright © *1986 Watterson. Dist. By UNIVERSAL PRESS SYNDICATE. Reprinted with permission. All rights reserved.*

First published by AuthorHouse 2/19/2009

ISBN: 978-1-4389-5259-8 (sc)
ISBN: 978-1-4389-5260-4 (hc)

Library of Congress Control Number: 2009900766

Cover Design by Scott Blow

Book Design by Beth Belcher

Printed in the United States of America
Bloomington, Indiana

This book is printed on acid-free paper.

Sacred Cow Company
www.sacredcowcompany.com

This book is dedicated to our biggest fans and supporters, our wives Noreen and Lee Ann.

Acknowledgements

We would like to thank the many people who helped bring this story to life and to print. Your help was greatly appreciated.

The teachings of those who pioneered the fields of behavioral science and organizational change have inspired our work, most notably: Richard Beckhard and Drs. Aubrey Daniels, Kurt Lewin, Jim Hillgren, John Kotter and B.F. Skinner.

We would like to recognize those who reviewed all or part of early manuscripts: Dr. Leslie Braksick, John Burden, Marcia Corbett, George Grenais, Bruce Johnson, Kirk Mandy, Ned Morse, Manny Rodriguez, Fred Schroyer, Derek Sidebottom and Dr. Julie Smith.

We are grateful for the wisdom and guidance of those who played key roles in getting this project refined and launched: Dr. John Brown, Ron Chalmers, Steve Jacobs, Betty Kennedy, Dr. Michael Miles, Beverley Patwell, Hilary Potts and Mark Ryski.

Thanks to those who had such an active role in the production of this book: our editor Claire Morris for her incredible attention to detail and for giving the manuscript a professional polish. To Scott Blow, a.k.a. cybermacgyver, for his creativity and patience while creating the cover artwork.

Very special thanks to our experienced guide on this journey: our triage editor Lee Ann Smith who helped keep our writing structured and clear, and who helped keep us motivated right to the finish line.

Contents

PRELUDE - Steve ... xi

PART 1: The Story - From Heyday to Mayday ... 1

CHAPTER 1: Things Have To Change - Geoff ... 3

CHAPTER 2: On The Outside Looking In - Steve ... 17

CHAPTER 3: On The Inside Looking Around - Steve ... 25

CHAPTER 4: Bring Me Data - Steve ... 33

CHAPTER 5: The First Shock Wave - Steve ... 49

CHAPTER 6: The Tucson Tape - Steve ... 55

CHAPTER 7: Quality And Time-To-Market - Steve ... 69

CHAPTER 8: The R&D Clock - Steve ... 77

CHAPTER 9: Sacred Cow Workshops: The Cow Patties Hit The Fan - Steve ... 87

CHAPTER 10: The Day We Touched The Moon - Steve ... 113

CHAPTER 11: Demo Day - Steve ... 121

CHAPTER 12: The Power Of Positive Feedback - Geoff ... 129

CHAPTER 13: After The Cows Went Home - Geoff ... 133

CHAPTER 14: Outcomes ... 137

EPILOGUE ... 143

PART 2: The Method - Tools And Techniques	145
CHAPTER 15: Principles, Models And Tools - Steve	147
CHAPTER 16: Understanding Behavior - Steve	151
CHAPTER 17: Framework For Organizational Change - Steve	161
CHAPTER 18: Some Thoughts On Theory - Dr. Michael Miles	183
CHANGE Assessment Worksheet	187
FOOTNOTES	191
BIBLIOGRAPHY	193
INDEX	195
ABOUT the Authors	201

Prelude – Steve

THIS IS A book about successful organizational change at a company called Mitel, one of Canada's foremost telecommunications producers. In two short years we led a large-scale effort involving over 500 people that improved company profitability by a multiple of 40 – from $2 million to $80 million.

Our roles in the story are very different. Geoff Smith was the Vice President of Research and Development, and was faced with huge organizational challenges. I was the Organizational Development leader hired by Geoff to help get the company back on its feet.

It would be nice to tell you that everything we did was planned and scripted and that all went according to plan. We wish we could tell you that everything we did turned out the way we intended. Unfortunately this is not so. But this is not a book about perfection. This is a book about action and about what really happened. What we did, what we failed to do. What worked, what didn't, and what we would do differently if we had to do it all over again.

The story spans 25 years of Mitel's history, but focuses on the two critical years during which the company was on the ropes. It presents three kinds of practical insights: Geoff's point of view as the "Change Champion", my point of view as the "Change Agent", and a company perspective on the business impact of our actions.

Part 1 of the book is the story of Mitel, which began as "the little company that could". As we tell the story of what led up to the need for change and how we implemented it, we'll point out "key learnings"

– important things that we discovered during the process. At the end, we'll summarize our thoughts on the "dos" and "don'ts" of organizational change as explained by the framework we used.

Part 2 of the book is devoted to the organizational change models we used, along with an analysis of how we applied them in practical ways at Mitel.

If you work for a company of more than 10 employees, we expect that you will see things in this book that you can relate to, as the types of issues we were facing are universal. We just seemed to be facing a lot of them all at once.

So whether you are reading this to change the entire direction of your company, build better products, help guide you through a post-merger integration or just improve the performance of your team, you will find proven ideas and approaches that can work for you.

Now, on to the story of Mitel…we hope you enjoy the ride.

PART 1

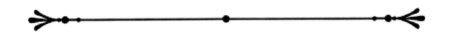

THE STORY:
FROM HEYDAY TO MAYDAY

CHAPTER 1

Things Have To Change – Geoff

ONE COLD DAY in January 1997, I was sitting in the boardroom of Mitel's headquarters along with the entire Senior Management team. Opposite us in this emergency meeting sat six of our most important customers, known as the "Elite Dealers' Council". These six people were the chosen representatives of the top 54 sellers of Mitel products in North America. This was a powerful and influential group and they were not happy. The group had demanded this meeting and there was only one topic on the agenda: product quality.

As the Vice President of Research and Development (R&D), I had known these people for a long time. They represented 80% of the revenue from our indirect distribution channel. We sold our products to the 54 dealers and they distributed them to end customers across North America. They also provided technical support to end customers and their message to us was crystal clear; they believed Mitel had released a new product too early. Problems were showing up in the field – problems that never should have escaped our lab-testing environment. The dealers felt that they were debugging our products at their own expense and at the expense of their customers.

The telephone business is a high-stakes game with little room for error. Any business without dial tone is like a company without oxygen. The very people who controlled the lion's share of our revenue were running out of patience with us and they were not going to continue to do business with us unless we got very serious about fixing these problems – fast. Without access to customers through these indirect distributors, we were done. Simple as that – Mitel could not continue to operate.

I was shocked. Not about the problems – for I knew these problems well, and the engineers in R&D had been working on solutions, although not nearly fast enough for the dealers. What shocked me was the realization of the impact that these problems were having on end customers and on the businesses of the dealers. To become an elite dealer these people were contractually bound to sell Mitel's products exclusively, so their business was essentially tied to ours. They could of course switch suppliers and leave us, but such a move would be hugely disruptive to their businesses. Their livelihoods were being threatened by our product problems.

Everybody in the room knew the same thing I did: this was squarely an R&D issue. It was my job to fix the products. The future of the company rested on my head and in the hands of my R&D department.

Things had to change.

***

When I joined Mitel in 1978 as a young electronics technologist the company was booming. Spawned by the deregulation of the telecommunications market, Mitel had the right product at the right time in the right place. The US government had just decided to deregulate the telephone companies (telcos), which meant that telcos no longer had a monopoly on providing telephone equipment to businesses. For the first time, businesses could purchase and connect their own, less expensive telecommunication equipment to the phone lines coming in from a telco. Mitel made complete telephone systems for small- and mid-sized businesses. They produced the telephone sets, small switchboards that receptionists would use, and devices called Private Branch Exchanges (PBXs).

Mitel Corporation was formed in 1973 in Kanata – a small city just east of Ottawa, Ontario, Canada. According to company folklore, the name Mitel is an acronym for Mike and Terry's Lawnmowers. When company founders Mike Cowpland and Terry Matthews left Northern Telecom (which would go on to become Nortel) and set up Mitel, they needed funds quickly so they decided to import and sell lawnmowers. As the story goes, the lawnmowers were lost in shipping and never arrived. In the meantime Mike and Terry secured their funding through personal friends and Mitel was born as a company.

The PBX is the brain of a telephone system and it has two main jobs. First, a PBX will link the telephone on a person's desk with an outside line and take care of functions such as hold, call forwarding, transferring calls and three-way conferencing. The second main job of the PBX is to save money. Many telephones spend a lot of time in idle mode. In a company of, say, 200 people, everyone will not be on the phone at the same time, so rather than pay monthly rent for 200 outside lines from a telco, companies use a PBX to juggle 200 lines on the inside of the company with as few as 20 outside lines rented from a telco. Mitel's SX-200, a PBX that could handle 200 inside phone lines, was the smallest, most feature-rich, and easiest-to-use PBX product on the market at the time. In 1978, sales of the SX-200 were on a rocket ship trajectory upwards.

Mitel's co-founders, Michael Cowpland and Terry Matthews, were true entrepreneurs who believed that absolutely anything could be done.

My interview at the company had begun by answering a typical list of questions by a Human Resources (HR) representative, followed by an electronics test. As I was puzzling over a schematic diagram, the door to the testing room burst open and in bounded a fellow I did not know. The test was timed, so I wasn't terribly interested in talking to this guy, but he asked me some questions about myself while I watched the time tick down. After he left, the HR person came in the room and said that my time was up. I handed her my incomplete test, figuring my chances of getting a job were slim.

Afterwards I was supposed to see either Mike or Terry for the second part of the interview process. My friends who were already working at Mitel had told me to hope for Mike – they said Terry was a wild man. As luck would have it, I was ushered into Terry's office and there sat the same guy who had burst into the room during my electronics test. I saw that he had the test on the desk in front of him and he asked me about the question that I hadn't finished. He began pointing out things that I should have considered in answering the question, and then suddenly he leaned forward on his desk and shouted, "Think man, think!"

It was my first introduction to organizational urgency.

The early days at Mitel were characterized by an air of "can do". We were all imbued with Mike and Terry's sense that anything was possible. Hallway conversations at the time were peppered with questions like, "Could you do it if your life depended on it?" – not as a threat, but to say you could do almost anything if you put your mind to it. It was a time of growth: we were hiring over 100 people a week and building factories around the world. We bought land in Bouctouche, New Brunswick, and Denver, Colorado, just in anticipation of future expansion. We purchased a semiconductor plant to supply our own microchips. There were executive jets and helicopters waiting to fly executives anywhere in the world at a moment's notice. Terry Matthews was known to have hung up from a phone call with a prospective client, then load our flagship product – an SX-200 – into the back of his car, go to the airport and fly to the customer's location. You can only imagine the look on the customer's face, finding Terry on the doorstep with an SX-200 in tow.

It was full speed ahead on all fronts and everyone was asked to give their all. Young employees were given large spans of control. New graduates were left with very little supervision and challenged to deliver sophisticated products. To everyone's amazement, products came out on time with strong features and functionality.

Before the SX-200, a state-of-the-art PBX was a large and cumbersome machine with mechanical relays. With all of its moving parts this kind of machine was difficult to maintain and upgrade. The Mitel SX-200 made history by becoming the world's first PBX to be fully software controlled and free of electro-mechanical parts. Like a modern day computer, the SX-200 could be upgraded with new features by simply adding or changing a software program. Meanwhile, competitors were changing circuit boards and mechanical components to achieve the same thing.

By 1978 – when our new headquarters building was being constructed and my "desk" consisted of a plank spanning two small file cabinets in a trailer out in the parking lot – Mitel had the dominant market share in the "below 100 lines" segment. (This refers to the number of inside phone lines controlled by a PBX.) We also essentially owned the hotel-motel market, and we were the dominant PBX player in hospitals and schools throughout North America and the UK.

As a company, Mitel attracted people who loved to take risks; innovative and very creative people – entrepreneurs at heart – who relished the chaotic yet euphoric environment of rampant growth.

The sun seemed to be shining so brightly on Mitel that few could even imagine dark storm clouds on the horizon. But big players were watching us closely. The larger companies were slow to respond, but eventually they did and over the course of 10 years they developed competitive products that rivaled all of the features and functionality of the once mighty SX-200. By the mid-1980s, the marketplace was crowded with competitors and a feeding frenzy began. The supply of PBXs began to exceed demand. With all the same features being offered, prices fell steeply as everyone began to compete on price.

We were a company in denial of the business reality around us. Entrepreneurial bravado had become an entrenched part of the culture and we still planned for future business based on the previous year's sales records. Mitel was now a victim of a phenomenon called "expense momentum". Even after the revenues leveled off, expenses ran high and could not be turned off quickly enough. Despite the fact that expenses were eating into the company's financial reserves, we continued to invest money into R&D in the hopes of finding the next big thing. If the SX-200 had been our ticket to the big time, a bigger PBX – the SX-2000, which could handle 2000 phone lines – would allow us to compete with bigger players by selling to bigger businesses. Unfortunately a bigger PBX came with more complexity and high R&D costs.

It didn't take long before Mitel was in dire straits or a "near-death experience" as many in the company referred to it. Now financially strapped, Mitel began looking for a buyer.

Telecom giant British Telecom (BT) came to the rescue, and bought a controlling interest in Mitel in 1986 for $217 million. This transaction marked the beginning of a new culture for the company. In order to pull it back from the brink, BT began to manage Mitel very differently than the entrepreneurial style of Mike Cowpland and Terry Matthews. The behaviors that had been reinforced in the company for years – risk-taking, innovation, and cost-is-no-concern – were no longer rewarded by the new BT management team.

The shift to conservative, risk-averse management was hard on entrepreneurs. Before long, the company's co-founders both moved on. Mike Cowpland left to form "Cowpland's Research Electronics Lab" (COREL) and Terry Matthews started Newbridge Networks. Many of Mitel's employees – the innovative, entrepreneurial risk-takers – quickly followed them.

Those of us who remained focused on getting Mitel restructured for long-term competitiveness and market staying power. We sold off surplus factories and real-estate holdings. Gone were the executive jets and helicopters. We tightened down expenses to reflect a company operating in a highly competitive market with slim profit margins. Everywhere we turned off the expense taps that were draining us. We had to reverse the expense momentum or the company was going to die.

This kind of significant emotional event shifted the company behaviors quickly and dramatically from an entrepreneurial style to a risk-averse style. Within a few short months, people were rewarded for taking a nickel out of the cost of a product rather than coming up with new ideas. We focused on process effectiveness and manufacturing efficiency. Everything was scrutinized and analyzed. Risk-taking was no longer in vogue.

The "little company that could" spent its first 10 years with its foot on the gas pedal. The next 10 years would be spent with both feet on the brakes. The company survived and eked out a respectable place in the telecom market. BT financed the final development of the SX-2000 and within a number of years the company returned to profitability.

About four years after the BT takeover, just as the sun began to shine on Mitel once again, dark storm clouds reappeared on the horizon. This time, the clouds were not of our making. The world of technology was fundamentally changing around us. Telephone systems had been around for over 150 years – almost five times as long as any commercial computer systems – but very suddenly the worlds of voice and data technology began to collide. It was becoming clear that you could use your computer network and wiring to handle both the data and telephone needs of a business. Data companies like Cisco and 3Com were touting the fact that they could provide voice communication over their data networks and you really didn't need a separate telephone infrastructure. Whether sending someone an e-mail or talking to them via phone, in the future both were going to be possible using one set of wires from the company's data network. Savvy business managers could envision cutting their wiring costs and support staff in half by combining voice and data, rather than supporting a phone system and a separate Local Area Network (LAN) data system.

As this new technology emerged, so did new roles and job titles. Telecom management used to be a stand-alone function in most companies. Now many telecom managers found themselves working for a chief information officer (CIO), who was typically responsible for two departments: the telephone department and the data department. CIOs most often came from a data background and had less knowledge of voice systems than data systems. The data companies already had a relationship with the CIOs, whereas companies like Mitel didn't. We suddenly found ourselves with less access to the decision-makers because we had relationships with the telcom managers, not the CIOs.

In their sales pitch, data companies like Cisco Systems were saying that if you bought their complete network solution, you were going to get voice communication for free. That sent shudders through the halls of Mitel. If this were true, then we had to do something, because voice switching was our entire business and it was in jeopardy of being wiped out.

The problem was that nobody – not industry analysts, not customers, not our Product Management team nor our senior managers – could predict how quickly the convergence of data and voice would occur. In fact, around the Senior Management table, a great debate raged about whether or not the PBX was dead and how much money we should put into developing a future PBX that could deliver voice-over data networks. Some people thought we needed to partner with a data company and just sell them our voice switching knowledge. Others thought we needed to compete directly with the data companies by running data over our systems, or develop a new system – a "Voice Over Internet Protocol (VoIP)" system – that would run on data networks. Still others doubted that the convergence would ever take place at all.

In 1992, while the discussion was still storming, British Telecom sold its 51% majority stake in the company to Schroders & Partners Ltd. of Montreal. Schroders installed a new President and CEO, John Millard, who in turn hired a fellow by the name of Ian Munns as senior VP Marketing and Technology. It was up to Ian to referee the great debate and set a course forward for us.

At that time I was the Head of Software Design in R&D and I knew two things. First, we didn't have the luxury to wait around and see what was going to happen; we had to decide, because big R&D development projects like VoIP can easily take five years to complete. Secondly, I knew that R&D was the product engine that had to keep the customers happy. Regardless of which decision we made – support the existing products, develop a new one, or both – R&D was going to be on the hook to deliver.

In R&D, you either build something or you don't; it's quite binary. There's nothing in between. It's all black and white – there is no grey. Unfortunately the world of evolving technology generates a "grey zone" and there is no crystal ball to give black-and-white answers. In the case of voice and data convergence we were facing a black-and-white decision based on something quite grey.

After many, many discussions with Product Management, customers, and outside analysts, Ian concluded that the convergence of data and voice would occur – but no one could predict how quickly it would happen. So there it was in all its grey fuzziness. A fundamental shift in the world of technology was coming but nobody could say how quickly. It was like standing on railroad tracks peering at the smoke puffing out of a locomotive headed towards us. How far away was it? How fast was it moving? Nobody knew.

We did decide a path forward but with great angst, because there were so many unknowns. We decided to hedge all bets and do both: Produce a new product that worked on a data network and continue with the existing PBX products at the same time.

Getting the balance right between developing the new and supporting the old was going to be a tough challenge involving both hardware and software teams. CEO John Millard decided to consolidate the hardware and software organizations and have them both report to me as the new Vice President of R&D. If we were going to undertake such an important new direction, John wanted to have the buck stop at one place: my desk. I now had an R&D team of 500 engineers; about 70% of them were turned loose on the challenge of building a new VoIP system.

***

Almost one year later, as the Elite Dealers' Council showed up and demanded an emergency meeting, I knew that we'd gotten the balance wrong. By responding to the fear that the data companies were going to take away our business, we'd taken our eyes off the ball and neglected our existing products. Now we were facing a group of our biggest dealers who had to be convinced to stay with Mitel. We later learned that Cisco was wooing them and trying to entice them to abandon us and distribute Cisco's new voice products.

All eyes were on R&D. After the emergency meeting with the dealers, the Senior Management team ordered another rebalancing of my organization to fix the existing problems in the field and get product releases back on track. We reversed the split of resources and now dedicated about 70% to current systems and 30% to the development of the family of new systems.

I had angry customers and serious quality issues in the field. There were new features to develop for our existing PBX products. Many of the engineers who had been working on the exciting new technology would have to be redirected "back" to working on the old, yet the PBX was dead – or was going to be, so I had to keep part of the team working on VoIP.

If we were going to compete in the data world it was a very different game. We had to speed up our software releases. Like most other PBX producers, we patted ourselves on the back if we came out with a release once a year while companies like 3Com issued new software releases every three months. On top of all that, we needed to design an architecture for the new VoIP product and we had a big knowledge gap in R&D. It had become clear over the past year that we just didn't have people who were experienced enough in the data world to build a VoIP product. The high-tech boom was scooping up talent all around us, so hiring was the most difficult it had ever been. We had to move quickly, but I was working in a conservative, risk-averse organization that had had the innovative spirit beaten out of it by the corporate "near-death experience" less than 10 years earlier.

Big things had to change. We had to improve product quality, we needed to work with technology that was new to us, and we had to do everything faster. We had to overcome all these challenges despite some ingrained, conservative behaviors.

We needed to transform the way that R&D worked.

I had three priorities:

- Fix product quality,

- Dramatically shorten our Time-To-Market, and

- Fix our talent gap.

In short order I became an evangelist to this cause, talking the dual mantras of Quality and Time-To-Market, talking about the future and what we had to do as a company to survive. I would explain over and over again how voice and data were coming together and how none of us would be around to work on that challenge unless we fixed the products in the field.

Mike Miles, a local professor of Organizational Development (OD) at the University of Ottawa, had been working with the Senior Management team, and John Millard suggested that I talk to Mike to get some insight into how Organizational Development could help us get to the root of the Quality problems and shift the culture of R&D. After an initial conversation with Mike, I decided that I wanted a full-time, dedicated OD person to help me reshape R&D. Two people in Mitel's HR department were interested in the task, but they couldn't meet either of my two critical requirements: devoting 100% of their time to R&D and reporting directly to me.

Dr. Mike was able to recommend someone for the role and that's how I came to know Steve Quesnelle.

Chapter 2

On The Outside Looking In - Steve

To put the Mitel story in proper context I have to explain how I came to work with my friend and mentor, Dr. Mike Miles. I began my career as an engineer at Canada's largest telco – Bell Canada. Shortly after I joined the company, Bell was deregulated and lost its monopoly in the market. Overnight the giant had to learn how to go from monopolist to competitor.

Within a couple of months of this shift, I found myself drafted to a team tasked with socio-technical redesign of Bell's ancillary businesses. A history of vertical integration meant that the financial results of these ancillary businesses were so tangled and interwoven that it was impossible to tell whether each was competitive on its own or not. On the "socio" side we were to get the employees ready to work in a competitive work environment. On the technical side we were to disaggregate or "de-vertically integrate" the businesses and get them packaged up to either operate in stand-alone business mode or be sold.

Part of my training for the role included an introduction to the profession of Organizational Development by Georgia consultant Larry

Miller during a Total Quality Management seminar. For me, all the light bulbs went on at that seminar as I caught a glimpse into the world of OD. It was all about communication, motivation and shaping key behaviors to achieve business results. As an engineer I was fascinated with machines, but no machine could ever match the intricacy of the human mind or explain the complexity of thought processes that become human behaviors.

To learn more about OD, I enrolled in nighttime MBA classes at my alma mater, the University of Ottawa. I opted to major in OD, and the first class I took was Organizational Behavior, taught by Professor Mike Miles. That class turned out to be the most important class of my life. Even past the end of the semester, I often found myself camped outside Dr. Mike's office door, waiting to discuss a journal article or work situation with him.

Just before graduating from the MBA program, I got a call from Dr. Mike telling me about a company that was looking to hire someone with my background. Mike was doing his own consulting work for Mitel and had met Geoff Smith, their VP of R&D. Here's what I recall him saying:

"Steve, you'll like this Geoff guy. He was the VP of Software Design at Mitel and has just been handed the Hardware team as well. With 500 developers and engineers now reporting to him, he wants a full-time internal OD person to help him make some changes to the department. They have their share of issues to deal with over there and I think this is a really good opportunity for you."

My next phone call was to Geoff Smith and 48 hours later I was seated in a Mitel boardroom talking to him. Every so often we have the pleasure of meeting special people – those who have an aura about them. They are the type of people who immediately put you at ease. They quickly get to the root of any issue and offer good advice in a way that makes you welcome it. You can talk to them about anything and always walk away feeling better about yourself. They are overflowing with self-confidence without ever a hint of overshadowing ego.

Dr. Mike was right: Geoff was immediately likeable. Within fifteen minutes of our meeting we were both standing by a whiteboard at the front of the boardroom. Geoff was drawing diagrams of their product release process and explaining the issues within his new R&D department. It boiled down to two basic problems: the engineering department was slow getting new products and features out to market and, when they did release something new, they were plagued with Quality problems. The Elite Dealers' Council had already made it abundantly clear that this could not continue. Mitel's Quality and Time-To-Market issues were leaving too many opportunities for competitors to nip at their heels, and Geoff was determined to put an end to both issues.

As Geoff explained it to me: "At the end of the day it really is an R&D problem. Sure we can point to Sales or Marketing and say, 'Hey, you guys oversold the customer,' but at the end of the day it is still an R&D issue. We are the product engine for this company and all roads lead back to us. What frustrates me is that we've got lots of smart people here but they just don't get it – our customers are really mad at us."

His energy and enthusiasm for the task were contagious. Of course recognizing a problem is usually the easy part. Doing something about it is another matter. A bit daunted by the size of the undertaking, I asked Geoff how he thought I could help him.

"You know, Steve," he said, "it's so messed up right now that you can come in and do anything. You can't possibly make it worse. You can only make it better."

At the beginning of our conversation, I got the sense that Geoff had been with the company for a couple of years. It seemed to me that he had been there for just long enough to understand the culture, understand the lay of the land and establish himself as a get-it-done guy. I was surprised to learn that he had actually been with the company for almost 18 years and had worked in various parts of the organization. It amazed me that after 18 years he still had a fresh outlook on things. He had taken on different roles in the company throughout his career and learned that there were two sides to every story. He had learned that it was not Sales or Marketing or Engineering or Manufacturing who was the enemy. The enemy was the competition outside the company – not anyone inside the company.

A few minutes later Ian Munns, senior VP Marketing and Technology for Mitel, joined us in the boardroom. Geoff thought it best that Ian have the chance to interview me alone so he excused himself. As it turned out, Ian was in desperate need of a cigarette break so the two of us walked through the parking lot as he interviewed me. I can't remember the questions that he asked, or any of my responses.

I just remember being scared throughout the entire walk.

Ian was not in very good physical shape and the walk was causing him to pant heavily. Amidst his panting he was puffing on a cigarette and I remember thinking, *Please don't have a heart attack out here in this parking lot or I'll never be able to explain it to anybody and I'll never get this job!* We did make it back into the building safely and, before showing me out,

Geoff explained that we had done things a bit backwards. "Interviews typically take place with HR first and then with the hiring manager but don't worry about it, we'll just have you back tomorrow to meet HR."

I left thinking, *"All right – I just landed a really cool job!"* Note to self: Don't count your chickens too quickly...

The next day I returned to meet the HR generalist for R&D. After 45 minutes of disconnected, uncomfortable questioning, I left thinking *"I better kiss that job goodbye."*

It was a foreshadowing of things to come. As a keen young manager, eager to put my new OD skills to work, I wasn't thinking strategically or else I would have asked myself: *Why is the Vice President of R&D hiring his own OD person? If I do get this job, how will it fit with OD's sister function, HR?* At the time I wasn't savvy enough to ask myself these questions, but the answers would become self-evident in short order.

A few days later I was surprised (and thrilled) to get a follow-up phone call from Geoff, asking me how the HR interview went. I told him that it had felt a little awkward and, in his typical "Geoff-aura" style, he assured me that it was nothing to worry about. The next day a job offer arrived at my house. My job title was to be "Head of Total Quality Management". Although the title sounded a bit odd, I didn't question it.

And so we were off: Geoff with his new department and customer challenges before him, me with my first lead role in a large-scale organization change initiative.

Geoff's Thoughts On This:

In order to get a dedicated OD person – who reported directly to me – into my organization, I had to fly under the radar and use a job title that fit within the R&D structure. Otherwise I knew that HR would stake claim to the role and my new OD person would end up being just another HR resource shared across the entire organization. I had big organizational problems to deal with and I needed full-time help. I had a Quality department that was in need of a leader, so ostensibly I hired Steve to manage our Quality department. One of our major problems was Quality, and he was going to be tasked with helping me fix it, so I thought it was a good cover. However, it soon became apparent to HR that Steve was not just a Quality manager but also much more.

Bringing in Steve to head up the Quality team led to some disgruntlement within the department itself. The department consisted of Ian and Bob – the keepers of our processes and technical Quality system. In reality these guys were auditors. Ian was a seasoned fellow and thought that he should have been given the manager's position. He had a hard time understanding how Steve could have possibly qualified over him for the job – he wasn't happy. I couldn't reveal that I brought Steve in for a much larger role without making public my bypassing of HR, and thus Steve was left to manage the situation.

HR soon saw Steve was doing more than managing the Quality department within R&D, which led to many discussions with my HR representatives as to what he was really up to. I was able to appease them – or so I thought – by explaining that Quality, in my eyes, went beyond testing and best practices, and was ingrained in the behaviors of the people in the department.

For a while I thought they bought it, but eventually I realized they hadn't. In retrospect it was a messy start; Steve had a disgruntled team to lead and the suspicious eyes of HR on him.

KEY LEARNINGS

Company

- Organizational culture is a powerful force and can be the demise of the company if not shaped in a healthy and productive way.

Change Champion

- Do what is necessary to get the resources you need.

- Make sure you understand the organizational politics.

Change Agent

- Organizational change will have the most success if driven by a line function rather than by a staff function.

- The first step in successful organizational change is to ensure there is a committed change champion in place.

Chapter 3

On The Inside Looking Around – Steve

On my first day, I arrived at work half an hour early and was ushered into HR with a batch of other eager recruits for our initial orientation. We had all been sent a package of information and forms with our offer letters. After walking us through the benefits forms, payroll deduction explanations, and other bits of paper, the HR rep asked us to take out the "yellow form" from our packets. The "yellow form" was our confidentiality agreement. She then asked if anyone had already signed the form. A few of us keeners put our hands up and were met with a scowl as clean forms were shoved our way along with the explanation, "I have to witness your signatures." I had been in the building for less than an hour and already I had angered the gods of "this is the way we do things around here".

Following the HR orientation, Geoff's assistant, Rosemary, showed me to my desk. After a trek to the supply cabinet we both noted that there was no file cabinet in my cubicle. Rosemary gave me a contact name in the Facilities group for furniture items. My next stop was Geoff's office for the inaugural office tour with lots of faces and names along the way. We stopped by to meet my "ISO Quality team"[1] (Ian and Bob) and all of

Geoff's direct reports. At the end of my tour Geoff asked if I was getting settled in okay and I said yes, all that I needed to do yet was track down a file cabinet. Geoff gave me the same contact name in Facilities and suggested that I do a walkabout of the floors on my own. Two hours later I found myself on the main floor close to the Facilities department so I dropped in to meet the folks there. I saw the person whose name I had been given standing by a desk peering intently down at a floor plan.

"Hi, I'm Steve Quesnelle. I'm new here and I understand that you can fix me up with a file cabinet," I said.

"You're the third person today to tell me that," she said in a monotone voice without looking up. She didn't say anything else or take her gaze off the floor plan.

"Great…I'm glad that the request has got through so quickly," I offered, not knowing quite what else to say. When she didn't say anything more or even look at me, I thought it best that I just move along. This was a sign of things to come from my friends in Facilities.

Back upstairs on the sixth floor I spent some time with my new team. Each of them was my senior by about 20 years. Bob worked part-time and was clearly the doer who maintained the ISO system. I could immediately see that he was going to be great to work with. Ian was hard to read. He had the air of a professional with a somewhat aloof academic bent. Geoff later told me that Ian had applied for my job and I suspect he was a bit annoyed at the prospect of working for this young "kid" who now stood before him as his boss.

Two days later, three people from HR dropped by my desk to introduce themselves and welcome me on board. Each of them had staff roles. One was the lead on training initiatives, and the other two were in charge of other HR programs and policy development respectively. Unbeknownst to me at the time, they all had their eye on the Organizational Development role and they too were curious as to why the VP of R&D had hired a manager of Quality with an OD background. They were full of questions about my thoughts and plans and how I intended to proceed. I wasn't quite sure of my diagnostic approach yet, and asked them to fill me in on their perceptions of the company. They shared three important pieces of folklore with me that day. First, they told me about the Elite Dealers' Council coming to town for the emergency meeting with the executives and how much pressure was on Geoff to get Quality issues under control. The second thing that they shared with me was a series of anecdotal stories about one of Geoff's directors, Brian, and his behavioral antics.

Brian was a colorful character in the department: a long-time employee, a quick thinker, and the man who was at that time in charge of R&D's Process Management and Product Validation. Brian was one of those characters with a larger-than-life reputation. He had his own special sense of humor and steely dark eyes that didn't suffer fools gladly. Brian was respected for his knowledge of the complex inner workings of the company and for his ability to outdraw anybody on any writing surface. From memory he would draw detailed diagrams, matrixes and flowcharts on a whiteboard until there was not a single square inch of white left. He was also feared for his quick temper, which had earned him an indelible place in the company folklore. As the story goes, at one point in his career – exasperated by the slow pace of a meeting that he was attending – Brian lay down on the conference room floor and kicked his feet like a frustrated four-year-old child.

The third anecdote that the HR folks shared with me was about an organizational change meeting a year prior. It had gone badly. Managers were flown in from various company locations – some as far away as the UK office – for the session. I didn't learn much about the content of the session, other than that the topic was organizational change. However, the feedback from the disgruntled managers at the end of the session focused on how "light" the session was. To paraphrase, they said things like, "We are all really busy people. You drag us all here for a couple of days that start late and end early. If you want us to come back you better be prepared to work us hard and long to ensure that we get value for our time." This was a highly important piece of feedback, so I filed it away for future use.

The impromptu visit from the three HR team members felt somewhat like a visit from a street gang. They had shared the pieces of company folklore as their way of saying that both the process issues and behavioral issues in R&D were grave – which was great. But I wasn't sure if they were telling me these things to prepare me or to scare me. My gut told me it was the latter.

While their stories were anecdotally interesting, I was going to need a lot more data before mapping out an organizational change plan. I filed their advice away in the back of my memory along with my earlier frosty reception in the Facilities department.

As I neared the end of week one, I went to the HR department to meet the HR director. I found her to be outwardly friendly yet somewhat guarded. During our first meeting, when I asked her to give me her sense of the Mitel culture, she told me, "It's a bit like a small town here. A lot of long-term employees and everybody knows everybody. We call it a FIFO culture."

Of course, FIFO is an acronym used in inventory accounting and computer memory space management. It means "First In = First Out". She must have noticed the puzzled look on my face and said, "FIFO… you know, Fit In or Fuck Off."

I wasn't sure if this was a blunt organizational assessment or some blunt advice to me.

Once again, it was a foreshadowing of things to come. During my time at the company I would visit the HR director in her office on many occasions. The key here is that I would visit her in *her* office. In six years, she only made one appearance at *my* office. In my naiveté, I didn't even see the battle lines being drawn and I wasn't picking up on the early subtle clues. Later I would describe it to people as being like a new puppy playing with the family cat. You know how puppies are forever tripping over paws that are too big for them, how they have non-stop energy to play, and the way that they just like everybody?

Then they meet the family cat.

The cat has been there longer.

The cat doesn't like dogs.

The cat has claws.

Still, the silly puppy keeps running up to the cat in the effort to play and, inevitably, keeps getting his nose scratched.

Welcome to my world.

Over time it would become increasingly evident that the HR department was as much of a detractor to the organizational change effort as any other department. Our performance management processes, compensation systems, and leadership development programs were all in need of an overhaul if we were going to turn the company around.

KEY LEARNINGS

Company

- For organizational change to be successful, OD and HR need to be aligned. The people systems, rewards systems, and performance management systems are key levers of change.

Change Champion

- Be prepared to be challenged by support organizations that yield considerable power.

- Do not waiver on what is important to you; focus your behavior on the goal you've set.

Change Agent

- Make note of every element of company culture and file them away until you see trends in the data that help to paint a comprehensive picture of the existing culture.

Chapter 4

Bring Me Data – Steve

GEOFF'S FIRST ADVICE to me was good advice. He said, "Spend some time with your team but don't get too far down into the weeds with them. Then just wander around and see what you can learn."

One thing was already clear to me – this company needed to make some pretty big changes. As Dr. Mike had once told me, "You only get one chance to make a first impression." There would be nothing worse than launching a major change effort that was off the mark and having to recalibrate and restart it. Big change makes people nervous, and they need to see strong, confident leadership at these times. Having to restart a change effort erodes all confidence and makes people even more nervous. This change effort was so big that I knew I was only going to get one shot at getting it off on the right foot.

By this point in my career as an OD professional I had already locked in on one central guiding principle: change for its own sake is misguided and irresponsible. Successful organizational change leads to a measurable increase in a significant business result in a way that employees want to, rather than have to, participate.

I had to really understand what I was dealing with at Mitel. Thus began my walkabouts to gather baseline data about the company.

Preliminary Observations: The Workplace, Meetings and Town Halls

The Workplace

I spent my first weeks on the job walking the floors, meeting people, and observing the way they interacted. R&D[2] was spread over three floors of an office tower in the sprawling Kanata campus. I remember being struck by the sense of quiet and decay. The carpets were worn. The fabric on the cubicles was a mishmash of various bright colors left over from the 1970s. Workspaces were piled high with circuit boards, test equipment, soda cans and paper. Bulletin boards in the hallways were layered thick with paper. When walking solo, people walked slowly with their shoulders drooped forward, something I came to call the "Mitel shuffle". When people did walk together – typically to or from the cafeteria – they appeared almost monk-like with heads bowed, speaking quietly and solemnly about deep technical subjects. It was obvious that there were strong cliques, and a pecking order of those who hung out together. Terry Matthews had left his legacy on the company with early recruiting practices: Mitel had a sizable population of people of United Kingdom origin, and Welsh in particular. This added another interesting dimension to the culture; you had to get to the cafeteria early on curry day or else you didn't get a seat!

Meetings

Another early element of the culture that jumped out at me was behaviors during meetings. Meetings are key to information-sharing and decision-making. I saw that both of these were broken. There are three common types of meetings: meetings to brainstorm and discuss ideas, meetings to make decisions, and meetings to share decisions. In R&D there was no distinction between what kind of meeting was being held, and good meeting behaviors were not practiced. I had believed the director of HR when she told me that Mitel was a lot like a small town. There was a certain familiarity across the company. Much like a group of squabbling siblings, I was appalled by the etiquette in meetings (or the lack thereof). Geoff's staff meetings would routinely become bogged down and unproductive by the amount of bickering, rhetoric, talking over one another, and general lack of listening. Meetings further down the management chain tended to be even worse. Mitel had a meeting-centric culture – a lot of time was spent in meetings and most of it was ineffective. Aside from the behavioral issues, there were a number of process problems as well. Too many people were involved in too many meetings, and decisions, when made, were poorly communicated. Often those without the authority to do so would make decisions – only to have them overturned in a later meeting by the true decision-makers, causing angst to both parties. The decision-making and remaking resulted in whipsaw behavior across the organization and was a sore point for all. When I asked Geoff about this, he agreed that the meeting-centric culture was problematic: "I think it is good that everyone who attends a meeting feels free to express their opinions but they don't understand that not everyone gets a vote."

People are, for the most part, consequence-driven, so I decided to try an experiment. I thought there might be some clues in the poor behaviors that I observed in meetings.

One evening I went to a dollar store and bought eight bright red space pistols. Plastic guns that made space-age-like whirring and zapping noises when the trigger was pulled (much like the soundtrack from a 1960s Martian movie). I brought the guns into our next staff meeting and placed them in the middle of the table.

"If you think someone is overstating their case, then feel free to zap them" were the only instructions I gave to the rest of the team. About half an hour into the meeting, Brian was on a roll with his theory of the day when fellow director Debbie zapped him. Brian stopped mid-sentence, and refused to say anything further for the rest of the meeting. My little experiment had provided me with an idea of what lever we could pull to change the culture: personal pride. Having personal pride at risk is a strong consequence and a powerful motivator. Now we just had to find the most positive way to use it to reinforce the behaviors that we needed. Meanwhile, the red pistols did have a slight ongoing impact at Geoff's staff meetings but we were still miles away from effective meeting behaviors.

Town Hall with the President

The large Mitel campus in Kanata had the luxury of a large open space that had never been developed. In the link between Phases 2 and 3 there was a cavernous hall that was to have become a new cafeteria to replace the aging one in Phase 3. The room was two stories high with a catwalk across the second level. After the near financial implosion of

1985, the new cafeteria was put on hold, and the company had wisely installed a PA system and large retractable screens in the space for the purpose of holding "Town Hall" meetings.

Town Hall meetings have different meanings in different companies: to some they are meetings with outside stakeholders (customers or shareholders) but to us at Mitel, it meant a large meeting between employees and the management team. I remember attending my first Town Hall – a quarter-end update by then CEO Dr. John Millard. John was a man of experience. In his early 60s at the time, he looked out of place amongst this high-tech crowd with an average age around 30. He stood on the podium with thumbs hooked under his suspenders, and spoke with a slight southern drawl, while his "lighten up this crowd" opening banter focused on fishing stories or the latest tale of his granddaughter.

John had the de facto respect that comes with the office of the CEO, but his image and body language failed to ignite the passion of his audience. It was a relationship that had all the love of an arranged marriage and was a vast departure from the invigorating fire-and-brimstone speeches that former CEO Terry Matthews had given from the same podium.

Preliminary Diagnostics: A Survey, Top-Down and Bottom-Up Data

A Survey

One day Geoff provided me with the results of an earlier study that Dr. Mike had done on R&D's culture. It was entitled "Around Here We Behave As If…" It was a fascinating summary of interviews with all of Geoff's direct reports and a cross-section of R&D employees. Dr. Mike had interviewed each of them about their role in the organization and once he got them at ease would pose the question: "Finish this sentence for me: "Around here we behave as if…" The results told of a team deeply fragmented, frustrated, and feeling disempowered to make changes. In fact, the majority of people responded, "Around here we behave as if its important to be nice." No-one confronted issues directly, inappropriate behaviors were tolerated, and decision-making processes were either missing or broken.

By now I was starting to swim in data points about my new employer's culture, but was still at a loss as to where to begin fixing business problems. For organizational change to be really successful, you have to start with a business issue and work backwards from there to figure out what behaviors are needed. There is no use jumping in and trying to change behaviors unless you can answer the question "So what?" "So what" is the business issue. Fixing a business issue will help sustain the new behavior. There were productive things that I could work on with this group – like their behavior in meetings – but I still didn't have a big measurable "so what" to work from at this point. I knew that "Quality" and "Time-To-Market" were the things that we needed to target, but I was still unclear on how they were being measured.

Top-Down Data: Red-Hair Diagnostics

I serendipitously dropped by Geoff's office one afternoon just to check in and I noticed an obvious change in his demeanor. His red hair seemed a little redder and his voice gruff. This became the first of many times that Geoff would vent his frustrations to me and provide me with the best organizational diagnostics that any OD professional could ever dream about. On this particular afternoon, Geoff was on a rant about "dumb things that keep getting done around here". There is an important distinction here: not dumb people, but dumb behaviors. The R&D culture was very procedure-driven, and once a procedure had taken root, it was too infrequently reviewed. It would continue, whether or not it still made sense. As Geoff continued his rant, I was awed at how such intelligent people could abdicate their cognitive powers all in the name of "following the procedure". If procedures don't make logical sense, there needs to be a mechanism in place to review and change them.

That afternoon meeting with Geoff was an epiphany for me. It gave me the toehold I needed to begin to scale the mountain of cultural change before us. Given his level in the organization Geoff could see the big picture across departmental lines. He also had a special gift of still being able to view the company with fresh eyes – he had not succumbed to what I call the Organizational Immune System™. [3]

The Organizational Immune System™ is the enforcer of current culture. As adults we have all developed our own protection systems. We might laugh when someone pokes fun at us to shelter ourselves from embarrassment. Like birds of a feather we flock together with friends and colleagues who tend to share similar beliefs and act in similar ways. It keeps life simple and it gives us some routine.

When you multiply similar thinking and similar behaviors across an entire employee population, the result is a kind of cultural inertia that we call the Organizational Immune System™. It is quick to chew up and spit out anything, or anyone, who is different or who wants to do things differently. It embodies the way that things get done, who fits in and who doesn't. The Organizational Immune System™ is forever morphing, changing to protect itself at all costs, but it never changes quickly. It grows slowly over time and is entirely self-serving. It is the Organizational Immune System™ that will have employees rearranging deck chairs on the Titanic. Organization culture is not a detractor to change; it is the Organizational Immune System™ that keeps the current culture from changing.

I realized I had to get Geoff to continue ranting to me. I was going to have to corner him every time I noticed that hair glowing red. With each new rant would come an insight into how the organization really worked and a new process or behavior to address.

Bottom-Up Data

Listening to Geoff's rants of frustration provided me with one mechanism for organizational reconnaissance, albeit a top-down and biased view. To round out my diagnostics, I was going to need a bottom-up view as well.

Eight years prior, while working as a summer student in a large, dirty industrial plant, I had observed something that I thought was brilliant. The workforce was a tough lot who belonged to a hard-core union. There was a lot of labor / management bad blood that went back two generations. The company also had a graffiti problem. The washroom stalls were constantly being defaced with graphic, raunchy graffiti. These guys were serious and it went beyond pencil, pen and marker – they etched their work directly into the paint and metal with nails and screwdrivers. Instead of a lot of scrubbing and constant repainting, the company decided that if you can't beat 'em, join 'em. Someone had come up with the idea of installing a 12 by 16 inch chalkboard (complete with a daily supply of fresh chalk) on the inside of every bathroom stall door.

Just like a textbook example of the "path of least resistance" theory, the bathroom artists found that it was easier and more convenient to draw on the chalkboard than on the walls of the stalls (not to mention the ability to use different colors!) so overnight the graffiti became confined to the chalkboards. Once a day the bathroom cleaning crews washed off the chalkboards and replenished the chalk.

Graffiti problem solved. No more scrubbing and painting.

I was amazed at the artistic talent of the blue-collar workforce. It was rude, crude and graphic, but incredibly clever and well-drawn. The daily mood of the plant could be read by taking a trip to the bathroom. I made a habit of going to the bathroom and reading the chalkboards in all of the unoccupied stalls every afternoon. You could immediately tell which supervisors were the most despised. It was a win / win for both sides: the graffiti problem was eliminated and the workers got an easier outlet for their frustrations. Unfortunately the company never addressed any of the employee issues and they eventually went out of business. It was too bad because all the data they needed was there in the bathroom.

I thought that this was an idea that I could somehow adapt to help me get "bottom-up feedback" (pardon the pun) at Mitel. Two months into my job, I opened the morning newspaper to the comics section and found a little gem. One of my favorite cartoon series was "Calvin & Hobbes". I believe in the power of humor as part of any intervention, especially during change interventions where things inevitably get tense at times. On this particular day, the cartoon showed Calvin's mother sweeping up a broken dish from the floor and chastising him for his seemingly careless actions. Her tag line was: "Don't you have any common sense?" Calvin's response, in his typical impish way, was: "I have lots of common sense – I just choose to ignore it!" This is exactly what we were facing – a bunch of smart people with lots of common sense, who were ignoring it – and I wanted to know why. I took my little cartoon and photocopied it on to a page with the following announcement:

Bring Me Data – Steve

Every large organization has a few skeletons in the closet - policies or practices that failed to evolve in a common sense way and over time these practices become a thorn in the side of progress.

Here at Mitel, we have succeeded in establishing some formal programs - like the PRTM initiative - to find and improve our processes, but there's always a way to do more. What we don't have, are very many informal channels to help us improve our culture, so that is the reason for this note.

I would like your help in finding out the things that we could change to help us work better. Things that can help us to help one another, things that can speed thing up.

Just take a yellow post-it note and put them here.

Unfortunately I can't guarantee that we can accomplish everything you post - but if can remove just one obstacle a month - we can make life easier for all of us.

Thanks,

Steve Quesnelle
Head of Quality Programs

Question of the week:

"What are some of the dumb things we do around here"??

CALVIN AND HOBBES © 1986 Watterson. Dist. By UNIVERSAL PRESS SYNDICATE. Reprinted with permission. All rights reserved. PRTM is from Michael McGrath, Setting the PACE® in Product Development: A Guide to Product And Cycle-time Excellence (Butterworth-Heinemann, 1992).

My hope was (à la the factory experience) that people would pen in responses to the questions. The original plan was to tape a copy of my mini-poster to the inside of the door on each bathroom stall. However, a significant percentage of our population was female, so that ruled out the washroom idea. I didn't want a reputation as the guy who frequented the ladies loo! As it turned out, the Administrative Services group was tasked with managing the content on all of the bulletin boards in the company but when I asked for their assistance to get the posters put up they politely declined the request.

In the end, Geoff's assistant Rosemary and I, armed with a roll of tape, put up copies of the poster beside each of the elevators on each of the six floors. Then I waited. After two painful days of silence I decided that my little experiment was a failure but left the posters up anyway. Then on day four I noticed a little yellow sticky note attached to one poster. On day five there were more yellow notes attached. The yellow sticky notes continued to show up and I gathered them up for two weeks before taking the posters down.

It didn't take me long to figure out why people posting sticky notes rather than writing on the blank space on each poster: nobody wanted to be caught dead standing in the elevator lobby writing on that poster. It was much safer to compose a response at their desk and quickly stick their thoughts on to the poster when no one was looking. The first rule of employee surveys says that if you want honest feedback from the front line, you have to make the process anonymous.

The delayed reaction was an important piece of data for me as well. This was a company and a type of work that attracted a high percentage of introverts. It took them a few days to think through what kinds of things they were going to attach to the posters.

There were a lot of repetitive issues on the sticky notes, but the most startling thing was the pettiness of the issues, such as: "Noise from nearby renovations is disturbing my concentration… The company job ads in the local paper are too boring… Give us free soft drinks… Send company-wide email when the library gets new books…"

There was griping and finger-pointing, but the overall trend was that people felt disempowered to make any changes themselves.

The poster exercise was very telling for me but not in a way that I expected. I had expected to gather good data about important things that needed to change. Instead of gathering data *from* the employees, the poster campaign allowed me to gather data *about* the employees. This was an organization that seemed to be deeply in the grips of learned helplessness – employees felt powerless to make changes so they gave up and griped about little things instead. It was going to take organizational shock therapy to break the bonds of the Organizational Immune System™. The conservative, locked-down, risk-averse stamp that British Telecom had put on the company during their ownership years had taken its toll on creativity and the ability to change. Outmoded processes and procedures were deemed untouchable and somehow "sacred".

Geoff's Thoughts On This:

Through my assistant, Rosemary, I was getting updates on what Steve was doing, as well as her take on his effectiveness. I always welcomed Rosemary's view as it was grassroots and to the point. She let me know that Steve was using interesting methods to determine what people were feeling and thinking about the company. That was all I needed to hear. I knew that Steve was not going to take a traditional survey approach to gathering the data necessary to evaluate the health of the organization. I have to say that when I heard Rosemary talk of putting up posters in the bathroom, I thought Steve had pushed a little too far. I was somewhat relieved to hear that the posters eventually went up near the elevators. One thing Rosemary and I both noticed was that Steve was using all his creativity to get the organization to speak to him regarding what they didn't like.

While Steve was integrating himself into the organization, I was doing a skills inventory. The entire 200-member Hardware Development team needed to be reorganized and reskilled for the task ahead. A similar retooling was required of the 300-member Software department. I hoped through the inventory to get a baseline of what skills we had and also to find talents already in-house that could help us. I thought that this was going to be a positive exercise for everyone in R&D. Unfortunately, it turned out to be a big waste of time. Those who wanted to work on the new product but didn't have the skills necessary, exaggerated their skill levels and experience. Meanwhile, those who felt threatened by entering the world of data feared that the skills inventory would be used to weed them out or marginalize them, so they too exaggerated. In the end, the exercise didn't yield anything that could be used to transform the R&D organization into a voice-and-data-savvy group.

What we ended up doing was asking each manager to assess the skills and knowledge of their team members. This built a much more accurate skills inventory, and did turn up a few positive surprises in terms of in-house talent. But there was not enough talent to close the skills gap. I knew we didn't have time to train people; we had to start recruiting people who had data knowledge. At the same time I had to keep the existing organization motivated and focused.

Key Learnings

Company

- Successful organizational change should always be focused on achieving an important business result.

Change Champion

- Learn to trust your OD specialist and accept the methods as viable even if you wouldn't do them yourself.

- Asking people to assess themselves when the personal stakes are high results in bad data.

Change Agent

- Be creative in your approach to collecting data and doing diagnostics.

- Don't react too soon to the data you collect. Look at both the data itself and what the data says about the way that people contribute the data.

- You need balanced – both top-down and bottom-up – data to get a clear picture of the organization.

Chapter 5

The First Shock Wave – Steve

GEOFF KNEW THAT in order to achieve his strategic objectives he needed to reorganize the R&D department. The organizational structure hadn't changed in five years; it was set up to sustain existing products only. So we began to plan our first off-site meeting to redesign R&D from the ground up.

We had to get his team of R&D directors to help design the organization so that some people could continue to work on the existing products and some would be freed up to work on the new product. Given the magnitude of the agenda topics, Geoff expanded the invitation list beyond his direct reports and invited 15 or so key R&D managers to the meeting as well.

We mapped out a full two-day agenda and booked the meeting at a local hotel and convention centre called The Barons. In retrospect it was a bit funny – "The Barons meeting" was just that; we had all of the R&D "barons" in the room together.

This was my first time facilitating Geoff's entire management team and they were a handful. The group had terrible meeting discipline.

When people were quiet, it didn't mean that they were listening; it just meant that they were waiting for their turn to speak. People interrupted one another or cut them off completely. By mid-morning on day two I was exhausted trying to facilitate meaningful discussion with the group.

At the morning break Geoff and I discussed the agenda and what to do next. We decided that the afternoon should be devoted to work in smaller group breakout sessions. Geoff asked me to run the afternoon session myself as he and the director of Software Design had to go back to the office and take care of something. I hadn't anticipated having to handle the group all by myself. They were tough enough to work with even with Geoff present, so I wasn't looking forward to the afternoon without him there. To my surprise the afternoon sessions went better than anticipated. I circulated between groups doing the best I could to keep them on track.

Just before the end of the session Geoff reappeared looking rather somber. I gave him a quick debrief on what I had the group doing and then asked what was up with him. I wasn't quite prepared for the bombshell that he dropped. He had gone back to the office to let the Software director go.

Boom – right in the middle of our first major reorganization off-site my new boss had fired one of his key lieutenants. Not just anybody, but the Head of Software Design!

When I asked what had happened, Geoff said that we needed to move the department in a new direction and he didn't think that the incumbent was the right person to get us there. Still reeling from the unfolding events I asked him what his communication plan was. He felt that there was no time like the present so we convened the entire group and he told them what he had just done.

The group got really quiet and stayed that way for a long time. I can honestly say that there was not one person in that room who could have anticipated Geoff's announcement. Actions speak louder than words and that afternoon Geoff sent a strong message to the entire department that it was time to get serious about operating differently. Until a replacement was found, Geoff would take on the role as acting Head of Software Design.

I give him a lot of credit for two things: firstly for making a really tough decision, and secondly for stepping up to the plate and filling the role himself until a replacement was found. Geoff's credibility as a "walk-the-talk" leader was cemented that day.

Geoff's Thoughts On This:

When I began to evaluate the skill gaps in R&D, I started by looking at leadership roles. The organization hadn't changed for so long, I felt that people were getting stagnant. To build new products we needed to think differently. Early in my career at Mitel I had been drafted from R&D to Manufacturing. This turned out to be a great experience for me because I learned what it was like to build things designed by R&D. I really got a sense of what it feels like to have things thrown over the wall at you. I could now see some of the same things happening within R&D itself so I knew that I needed to move some people around and get them standing in one another's shoes. I needed to stretch people and get them thinking, learning, and co-operating between groups in new ways.

On the Software side in particular, I needed someone who had data experience, especially voice and data working together. Unfortunately the incumbent didn't have this skill set, so I planned to have him look after the traditional products and then hire a new person to look after the development of the new product line. I thought at the time that I was going to split the role between maintaining the old and developing the new, because I felt that the two groups needed to be motivated differently. But when I approached my Software director about this idea he wasn't too keen on it and we couldn't come to an agreeable compromise. So I thought it was best if we parted ways. I have learned that no one person is irreplaceable. Yes, it may take some time to get back on track, but in the end you gain more respect from the organization by being decisive, and demonstrating your commitment to achieving what you are saying.

The other managerial philosophy that I stick to is that the best way to determine what qualities and characteristics you're looking for in a particular position is to put yourself in that chair. So I assumed the role as acting Head of Software Design.

This change created what some people called a "shock wave" through the organization. It showed that I was pretty serious about retooling R&D and I wasn't worried about letting people go in order to get it done. A few months later I decided that we needed to replace the Head of Hardware Development as well so I personally spent a lot of time recruiting to get the two new directors we needed to help develop our future products.

Key Learnings

Company

- Establish policies that allow people to move around. They need to experience what it feels like to work in other departments to avoid complacency and improve their perspective.

Change Champion

- Always walk the talk. Be prepared to make tough decisions and show that you are serious about change.

- When you ask people to take on new roles, do new things and do things differently, expect resistance! Express confidence that they can do the new job and give them the support they need to succeed.

Change Agent

- Always be prepared to roll with the punches. Organizational change can precipitate sudden, unexpected turns.

Chapter 6

The Tucson Tape – Steve

AFTER SOME INITIAL data-gathering I was beginning to see two systemic issues that were impacting Quality and Time-To-Market. The first issue – which Geoff called "the spaghetti syndrome" – was affecting product Quality. The second issue was "feature creep", and it was delaying the release of new products and bug fixes.

The "spaghetti syndrome" was based in the reality that it takes millions of lines of software code to make phones work. Our products had been around for a long time, and the code had passed through the hands of many different software developers throughout the years, each with their own style of writing software. As Geoff would describe it, "When it comes time to introduce a new feature into the call control software it's like working on a plate of spaghetti – you pull something over here and something else moves on another part of your plate." Introducing a new feature in one part of the call control software often had the effect of breaking another feature elsewhere in the code.

The other problem – "feature creep" – was based on the struggle of figuring out whom to listen to when it came to deciding whether or not to include a new feature on a product. Mitel had multiple sources of input and conflicting priorities: the Sales and Marketing people wanted to mirror every feature available on competitors' equipment; the Product Line managers wanted to generate the largest return for the lowest amount of engineering time to build a feature; and of course the R&D engineers wanted to design and build cool features whether or not there was anyone out there who would pay for them.

Wrangling between these three stakeholder groups resulted in this phenomenon called "feature creep". Rather than cut things out of a specification, additional features tended to creep in, which delayed the launch date. It seemed as though a specification was never really locked down. There was constant grousing about what the priorities were and how often they changed.

Geoff was adamant that the voice of the customer was too far removed from R&D to fix either problem.

Having experienced three or four "Geoff rants" about the voice of the customer being absent from R&D, I started to think about how we might address this problem and therefore start to deal with the spaghetti syndrome and feature creep.

We were lucky to have a strong dealer network. Even better was the fact that they met twice a year to gang up on the company and show their teeth. Mitel actually arranged the dealer meetings both to hear from them and to showcase new products and ideas that we had in the pipeline. The dealers would meet by themselves on the first day, and a cross-section of Mitel leaders from Sales, Marketing and R&D would participate in the second day of meetings with them.

As the March dealer meeting in Tucson, Arizona, approached, I got an idea. I bounded into Geoff's office with that "I've-just-discovered-the-meaning-of-life" look in my eyes and proceeded to make my pitch. Geoff and I had developed pretty good rapport by this time so I began by trying to twist him up a bit just for fun.

"Hey! I've got this great idea. The next dealer meeting is in Tucson so I thought I'd take R&D along. You know… dip them in the river of customer experience. So, waddya say? Can I have 500 airplane tickets to Arizona?"

Recognizing that I was poking fun, Geoff just pushed his reading spectacles further down his nose and peered at me over the top of them, not saying a word.

"OK, OK, so how about this – I'll bring all the dealers here to Kanata. We can have the meeting here and they can spend some time enjoying the Canadian winter for a few days. Can I have 100 plane tickets to bring them in?"

Still silence and more peering over the top of his reading glasses. I suspected that I had better pick up the pace of my sales pitch as I noticed his red hair glowing a little bit brighter.

"All right, all right, you've got me, so here's what I was really thinking. I can combine those two ideas for the price of one plane ticket."

Maybe he thought that if he looked interested in one idea that was a little less hare-brained, I might go away. "OK, now you're talking – what's the idea?" Geoff said.

"What if I go down there and rent a meeting room beside theirs? I'll grab them one at a time and interview them on videotape with a short list of really open-ended questions – easy things that they all have an opinion on and not too deep so as not to put them on the spot. Then we can edit the tape down and show it to all of R&D. We can connect our folks directly to the voice of the customer. Let them all listen to the pain that Quality and Time-To-Market is causing the dealers."

It was agreed and we worked on the list together on the whiteboard in Geoff's office. Within an hour we came up with 10 questions:

1. Do you perceive Mitel to be a market leader in the industry?

2. What do you think are Mitel's two major strengths?

3. What do you think are Mitel's two major weaknesses?

4. How satisfied are you with the Quality of the Mitel product line?

5. Who do you consider to be Mitel's major competitors?

6. Have you noticed any changes at Mitel over the past years in the areas of Quality and Time-to-Market?

7. How has your company done in the past year as a result of Mitel?

8. How does your relationship with Mitel compare to that of other suppliers?

9. What are the two top things R&D could do to double your sales?

10. What would you like to say to the R&D employees in Kanata?

Our strategy was to ask them easy (but pinpointed) questions in a manner that was open enough to allow them to steer their answers towards the pain points of their own particular business. We didn't tip our hand to let them know that we were coming or that we would be packing video gear. We didn't want to give them a chance to think about it and decide to back out. Neither did we want any political posturing or slickly crafted messages – we wanted to put them on the spot to get the gut reaction and passion of small company owners who were our business partners.

As a footnote to this story, booking the travel, hotel and conference room were all easy, but I was missing one important ingredient – a video camera. I checked out the rental prices with various audio-visual rental companies and then went to the Yellow Pages looking under pawnshops. The next day I purchased a small VHS video camera and tripod at a local pawnshop for less than the price of a four-day rental. Geoff always thought it was funny that I had done this but I always treated the company's money like my own and looked for easy ways to stretch a buck.

Videotaping our dealers turned out to be one of those spur-of-the-moment ideas with a result that would become a defining moment in company history. I had wanted to drop a small stone into the culture pond in the hope that small ripples of change would begin to move across the organization. We were about to toss in a boulder.

A week later in a Tucson conference room, Ken Dumont, our VP of Marketing, offered the company welcome at the dealer meeting. Ken introduced me and told the dealers that I would be asking them to meet with me for brief interviews. I had set up the room next door as planned: two chairs – one for my interviewee and one for me. The video camera on the tripod was positioned to peek out just past my left shoulder in the hope that my interviewees would forget about it and speak candidly to me.

My first interview was with Gene Collins – a successful New York dealer. Like many New Yorkers, Gene was not a shy fellow. He was also an influential thought-leader with his fellow dealers, so I picked him to be the first to join me next door. When I went into the meeting room and tapped him on the shoulder he immediately obliged for "a 20-minute interview".

When we arrived next door and he saw the camera he became immediately cautious. "Hey, what are you going to ask me?" he quizzed.

I handed him a copy of the 10 questions that I had printed off in large print. After reading through the list, he eased up a bit and said, "OK, I can answer all of these. So I guess you are making this tape for your senior managers?"

"No, Gene, we've got Kenny and Carl, Geoff and Ian, in that room next door with you. Our big brass are all there."

"So you want something for your middle managers?"

"No, we've got Paul Lanigan, Steve Lyon and Paul Lennon over there with you too."

"OK, I give up. Who are you making this tape for?" Gene asked.

I didn't really know how far to go with an explanation, but I had always been taught that honesty was the best policy. And so I explained to Gene that Geoff felt that R&D was really missing out on the "voice of the customer" and that we were going to show the tape to all of R&D along with anybody else in the company that we could drag into the room.

Gene is a pretty big guy. He came right over and looked me in the eye. "So you are going to take this tape – take exactly what I say and show it to your engineers?"

"Yep," I assured him.

He got this big smile on his face and said, "You know, Steve, I only deal with two companies – you guys and Toshiba. They're never going to send somebody all the way over here from Japan to make a video of me for their engineers. Roll that tape!"

I'm not sure what Gene said to the group when he rejoined their meeting next door but for the rest of the day they came in, one at a time, and spilled their guts. They spoke glowingly about the things they liked; they practically spit fire when they spoke about their pain points. We were several thousand miles from Kanata, but these dealers had a great deal of insight into the way we did things. They named Mitel employees as they told their stories. You could see the passion in their eyes and hear it in the timbre of their voices. By day's end I had four hours of video that would become edited down into the legendary Tucson Tape.

I flew back home Sunday morning and by mid-afternoon I had cobbled together two VCRs in my living room to begin making a rough edit by stringing all the responses to each of the 10 questions together in sequence. The result was a 40-minute tape. It was rough and really choppy, given the crude editing method, but I gave Geoff the copy on Monday to take home and watch that night as a sample of what was to come. Much to my surprise, he loved it just the way it was. He thought that the choppy "homemade" editing job added to the authenticity of the tape. This was not a slick, glitzy marketing piece – this was more of a rogue insiders' documentary focused entirely on the content. We had our own reality TV show!

Geoff had me book a meeting room for the entire day on Wednesday, and we started to gather people up, 50 at a time, to watch the tape. Geoff emceed each meeting, and told the audience of engineers that he thought the voice of customer was really missing from our decision-making. He told them that following each dealer meeting, the company people who attended would come back and brief others on what had transpired, but that the true passion of the dealers didn't get inside the company. Geoff told them about the list of 10 questions that we had asked the dealers, and told them that they were about to see and hear the responses on the tape. He warned each audience that they were going to hear some things that they would like and some things they would not like. Then he would hit the play button on the VCR.

It was fascinating to sit at the back of the room and observe the body language as people watched the tape. It was obvious that many people were surprised at the amount of insight the dealers had into the way that we worked — just as I had been. Many people had heard the names of these dealers, and some had even talked to them on the phone, but very few had ever met them or even seen their faces. And here they were in living color. As dealers would name individuals from Tech Support or other areas that had been helpful to them you could see members of the audience sitting a bit taller in their seats. Others would shrink down when singled out by name as unhelpful or unresponsive. All in all you could not sit in that room without being swept up in the day-to-day frontline experience that these dealers were living. We were doing dumb things that hurt their business and without them there was no need for us.

After each viewing of the tape, Geoff asked the audience for their reaction and spent time answering their questions. "What do we need to do to fix this?" "Is Geoff mad about what the dealers said about us?" "What are his first priorities for us?" There were essentially two responses to those sessions: people either ran out of the room quickly at the end to get back to their desks to start doing something about what they had just heard, or else they flocked around Geoff and me to tell us why the customers were wrong. I remember one particularly animated individual explaining to me that "software is an art of creation and you can have it fast or you can have it good but not both." It was really easy to see who amongst our herd needed the most help. As Geoff took to saying later, "We can carry our wounded but we'll shoot any stragglers."

As word of the tape spread around the building, we held further sessions at the request of other groups who wanted to join in. People from Sales, Marketing and even Facilities Maintenance wanted to see this tape that everyone was talking about. As an OD professional, you know you've hit the right target when people start asking to climb on board. Of course we had our skeptics too. Those who had the chance to interact with the dealers complained that we were making a big noise about old news. Of course, they were half right – it was old news. But it was worth making a big noise about. In retrospect, we had stumbled upon a hyper-effective way to get the right message into the right hands and minds quickly and without any filtering. In retrospect, regarding "stragglers", we should have fired a few more warning shots earlier based on some reactions to the tape. While I don't have the actual data, there was a strong correlation between those who hung around to tell us that the customers were wrong, and those who would leave the company over the next 12 months – either voluntarily or otherwise.

As children we used to play something called (ironically) the telephone game. Everyone would stand in a circle and the first person would whisper a sentence to the person beside them. The message was whispered around the circle from ear to ear and the last person would announce what they had heard. The first person would then say what the sentence started out as – usually with hilarious differences. I wanted a real-life example of this game to use as part of my orientation presentation to new recruits so I enlisted my sister Gail, a kindergarten teacher, to help. My favorite example of the telephone game from her class started out as "Santa wears red silk pajamas" and came back around the circle as "the chicken sits on a saw". As I would tell that story at orientation, people would laugh, but it always made a good segue into the "telephone game" that gets played every day in organizations. I would show the new recruits a few minutes of the Tucson Tape and encourage them to always be on the lookout for ways to get firsthand, unfiltered, information.

Geoff's Thoughts On This:

I had heard a phrase from Michael Hammer, when he talked about reengineering the corporation. He talked about change and people who wanted to change and people having difficulty with it and needing some help, and others paying lip-service to it, saying *yeah, yeah, yeah, we'll change*, but meanwhile thinking there's no way they're going to do it; they think they're going to outlast you somehow. The phrase he used to indicate to people he was serious about it was: "We're going to carry our wounded – and shoot the stragglers." I thought what a great phrase, because you know, if people want to change but are having trouble with it, we're going to help them through it. However, if you're going to sit there and take pot shots, we're going to take you out. Since I'd released a couple of people in the organization, they knew I was pretty serious about making those drastic changes. So that was a real awakening for people inside the company when they heard me say that.

Sometimes R&D people get somewhat calloused in their view of what happens out in the field because they believe customers don't use the product properly, or aren't as smart as they are, therefore making their own problems with it. But out in the field, these people were making a living selling and supporting Mitel products. When things got off the rails it affected their livelihood and their ability to sell products because of the reputation that the products don't work. R&D people, through all the various layers of management between themselves and the Sales, Product Management and Field Service organizations, are isolated from the field. We wanted to see if we could bring the voice of the customer into R&D. It's been a saying in every company: they say they want the voice of the customer inside the company, but how were we going to do that for 500 people?

Steve came up with the idea that he'd go out and videotape interviews with the dealers.

They said things like "cannot continue in business"; they talked about the errors in the product; about what they thought of R&D people and what it meant to them personally in their business, and it was right out of their own hearts, you could see it on their faces. In that room for 40 minutes there was dead silence. People were riveted to this video. It was a galvanizing moment, for sure. The dealers were talking directly to them, telling them what they thought about the product they were currently installing and what they thought about the engineers' ability to fix it.

It was probably the best way to get the voice of the customer into the R&D people's minds, because after that, things changed dramatically inside the company. We used to allocate resources to fix a problem, but there were always conflicting priorities. After that video, fixing problems became much higher in the consciousness of R&D.

But we still needed to learn how to act on it.

Key Learnings

Company

- It is vitally important to get the voice of the customer inside your company.

- The *best* voice of the customer is unfiltered and simple.

Change Champion

- Getting the voice of the customer inside the company is a win-win. It is good for you to hear it, and never underestimate the customer's desire to provide it – they want to give you information about things that will help their businesses too (which builds loyalty).

Change Agent

- Look for simple and timely ways to get the unfiltered voice of the customer into the company.

- Mine for the few big nuggets – such as trends in the information – to unearth the most important things that matter to the customer.

CHAPTER 7

Quality And Time-To-Market – Steve

ABOUT TWO MONTHS after the debut of the Tucson Tape, Geoff had another rant. We had a customer who owned a golf course and had set up his telephone system to let members phone in and book tee times using an automated feature in our software. The customer loved the application but had encountered a unique bug that kept resetting his telephone system – hence putting it repeatedly out of commission while it reset itself. Given the business impact of his problem, the bug had been escalated to Geoff, who was monitoring the fix. After not hearing a progress report for a couple of days, Geoff went down to the lab to get an update. A technician told him that they had written a software patch to fix the problem and they were just waiting for the Quality Assurance (QA) team to test the fix. After a bit more digging, Geoff found out that the person scheduled to do the QA was away on vacation for a week so the patch was going to sit on the shelf until the person returned. After issuing some quick "suggestions" on getting the patch to the customer immediately, Geoff stormed into my office.

"Can you believe it? They have a patch written and it is sitting on a shelf until one QA guy returns next week! R&D is throwing things over the fence to Quality Assurance and assuming that everything is OK if they don't hear anything back. There is no follow-through or accountability to the customer. While the patch is sitting on a shelf this poor golf course guy is left in the lurch! If they think they have the problem solved, ship it! Better yet, get on a plane and deliver it in person and stay there to see if it works or not. I don't get it Steve! Why do our people still have no sense of urgency about this stuff? I mean, we're coming into the weekend and we've got this poor customer out there trying to run his golf business! When do they think the big demand for golf tee times is?"

And with this rant another idea was born. Clearly we needed more attention on bug-fixing, and the R&D team lacked a sense of urgency to get things out the door quickly – both new things and bug-fixes.

It was around this time that we had all been reading Jim Collins' book *Built to Last*.[4] Geoff and I took away two different messages from the book. Geoff particularly liked what Collins referred to as "the tyranny of the OR versus the brilliance of the AND". This was exactly the problem that our Tucson Tape naysayers couldn't get past. They were stuck in the tyranny of the Quality versus Timeliness battle. We had to be smarter and find the brilliance of the AND – doing things quickly *and* doing them with high Quality. The thing about the book that I enjoyed the most was reading about the commitment of leaders and the importance of leaders "walking the talk". I knew that Geoff and I would be successful because as our "Change Champion" he continually did things to personally lead change.

One of the big takeaways from the book that Geoff and I shared was what Collins refers to as the concept of a "BHAG (Big Hairy Audacious Goal)" as a rallying cry for action. After pondering the idea of a BHAG for a few days, I went to see Geoff. I was still looking for a clearly measurable business goal as an anchor for behavior changes.

"Hey, if you had a magic wand, what bug would you do away with first?" I asked.

"Mate-link," Geoff replied without missing a beat. "We've had this mate-link problem with the SX-2000 for too long now and I don't think anybody is bent out of shape about getting it fixed."

So then and there we hatched a plan to hold an R&D Town Hall with one topic on the agenda: timely bug-fixes. Our example, our poster-child bug, was going to be the mate-link problem. I put on my behaviorist hat and worked with Geoff on how we would position this initiative. I wanted him to inspire them with the BHAG and the bragging rights that would go to the one who broke this bug, rather than to chastise them for their poor progress to date. To underscore the importance of this we offered a carrot: $1,000 to the person or team who could crack the bug in two weeks.

The next day, with 500 engineers and technicians assembled in the Town Hall area, Geoff stood at the podium. Without accusing anyone, he started with the golf course story and went on to tell the crowd how there was something wrong with the way that we worked. We were "throwing stuff over the wall" and assuming someone was there to catch it. In this case, nobody was home on the other side of the wall (QA) and the bug-fix was doomed to wait — at the customer's expense. He told them about the tyranny of the OR versus the brilliance of the AND

(Quality AND Time-To-Market) and then he threw down the gauntlet: there would be a bounty for cracking the mate-link bug.

As he always did, Geoff opened the floor to questions before wrapping up the Town Hall meeting. As an extreme extrovert, Geoff's passion and rapid-fire flow of information would often exceed the absorption capacity of his largely introverted engineering audience. Geoff would often complain to me about the lack of audience interaction, but on the other hand he wasn't very comfortable waiting for his audience to contemplate the content and formulate a response either.

On this day there were no questions and as the group did the "Mitel shuffle" out of the room they seemed even more reserved than usual. I was puzzled at the lack of positive response to our challenge. Geoff had done a really good job of communicating one of our key pain points without beating up any individual or group. We had tossed a really good BHAG to this smart group along with a nice carrot. Perplexed by the almost somber reaction, I took one of my engineering buddies to lunch and asked for his thoughts on the flat reaction.

"Well, you know, Steve, it's not as though nobody's tried to crack the mate-link…and…well, it's not a new problem," he said. "It has actually been around for a couple of years now and the code is so complex we just don't know what is causing it."

I was mortified. Was our first BHAG about to go bust? One thing that I had learned about the culture was that it was cynical and didn't suffer fools gladly – less so fools in high places. Had I just set Geoff up as the emperor with no clothes – a leader who was out of touch with the reality of what was happening within his own department?

Our two-week deadline came and went quietly. I was relieved to find out that between the impact of the Tucson Tape and Geoff's impassioned "Tyranny of the OR" speech, people were starting to get the message that our Quality issues were being watched by all of the really important stakeholders.

But the mate-link bug clung to life.

Geoff's Thoughts On This:

Steve and I were trying to keep some simple, very focused messages in front of the R&D team. My mantra became: "Quality *and* Time-To-Market." It's an AND function, not an OR function. We started this whole campaign of change management in the R&D organization, where the theme was "Quality *and* Time-To-Market." It was important to have a theme because it helped to keep the messaging simple. You could introduce new processes, new technologies – and every time I spoke I talked about Quality and Time-To-Market – to the point where I thought people were getting pretty sick of hearing me talk about it. Nonetheless I continued to go down that road and continued to emphasize the fact that we had to do things differently. It is really important in a time of change to keep the big picture in front of people or else they'll easily stray. We had to look at our new competitors as the competitors of the future, and we could not have Quality issues with new products coming into the marketplace. We had to do it quickly and we had to meet our customer Quality quantitative measures.

Every time we had a Town Hall meeting I would talk about my mantra, and we started looking for ways in which people could step up to this. We decided that we had to talk about some of the key issues and institutionalized behaviors that we had to change. What we needed was to get people to try new things and to take responsibility for Quality.

KEY LEARNINGS

Company

- It is not possible to keep focus on doing too many things at once. Pick your one or two biggest business problems and go after them. Keep focused.

Change Champion

- Learn what motivates your organization and use it as a consequence. Money doesn't always work; in fact, it usually doesn't.

- Keep the big picture in front of everyone, even if you think they're sick of hearing it.

Change Agent

- If you are going to use a BHAG as a rallying cry for action as part of an organizational change effort, be sure to do your homework first and select something that is achievable. A stretch goal is good, but it must be achievable.

Chapter 8

The R&D Clock – Steve

Geoff continued to offer up good information as we commiserated about the organization's ills. One day he showed me an email that our CEO John Millard had received from an angry customer who claimed that he was "going to rip out your system and throw it into the street and I'll tell you why…" I slipped a copy of this little gem into my diagnostics file and knew that it would come in handy someday.

Another of my favorite documents surfaced in a staff meeting. Geoff arrived in a terrible mood with a copy of the latest update from the Project Management team. He challenged his team on their knowledge of the status of projects under development: "Have you seen the project management list lately? Every one of our projects is running late!"

Earlier I said that change for its own sake is misguided and irresponsible. Successful organizational change leads to a measurable increase in a significant business result in a way that employees want to, rather than have to, participate. For organizational change to be really successful it is crucial to start with a business goal and work backwards from there to figure out what behaviors are needed to achieve the goal.

We only had two big issues in R&D: Quality and Time-To-Market. It suddenly hit me that the project management list was the business measure of Time-To-Market.

We had adopted the PRTM process for getting projects evaluated and completed quicker. This process was taking root, but our problem was still a prevailing blasé attitude about delivery timelines.

I found myself thinking about the year 2000. As the world marched towards the new millennium, a large number of unique projects had popped up around the globe. It seemed that every city had at least one big clock somewhere counting down the "days to Y2K". All this focus on time gave me the idea that maybe we needed an R&D clock of sorts – one that counted down the time that it took us to deliver projects.

Project deliverable times were measured in months and weeks. But we don't live a month or a week at a time. We live day by day. Our hearts beat and we take in breaths of air in seconds. Converting each of our project deliverable dates from months and weeks to a number of days was pretty simple math. For example, if a project was due on May 18th then the project was due to deliver on the 138th day of the year.

My plan was to build a huge digital clock with segments that would display the day of the year, hour, minute, second and tenth of a second. Below the clock we would mount a bulletin board listing all of our projects and the day of the year that they would be completed. On the left-hand side of the clock, things would move pretty slowly, as the day counter only changed once every 24 hours. Similarly, there wouldn't be a lot of rapid activity on the hour counter. However, on the right-hand side of the clock, the tenths of seconds would scream by so quickly that they would be hardly visible to the naked eye and beside the tenths of seconds would be the seconds counter clicking by in rapid succession. The message of the clock? Time is flying by – just look over to the right! Remember the old saying, "Look after your pennies and the dollars will look after themselves"? If we took care of the seconds better, the weeks and months would look after themselves.

Since we had a large team of electronic wizards in R&D, we decided to build the clock ourselves. Unfortunately, there was no sense of urgency to get the project done and the design team informed me that their time was consumed by revenue-generating projects for customers. Clocks were not the forté of telecom engineers, after all. After two weeks of no progress on the clock project, one designer stopped by my desk with some Internet research he had done. He had located a company called Applied Technical Systems that specialized in custom-made digital clocks and he suggested that I give them a try.

I phoned Applied Technical Systems and described what we were looking for. They didn't usually do clocks that counted either days or tenths of seconds but were sure that they could adapt their electronics to do both. After a quick budget approval from Geoff (as I was now taking the project outside of the company) we had a deal. The next day I faxed the company a hand-drawn sketch of what we wanted, along with some rough dimensions and a request for bright red digits, each about a foot high. We wanted this clock to be noticeable. A mere 11 days later an eight-foot-long box arrived at my desk via courier. The R&D clock had arrived but I was soon to learn that the Organizational Immune System™ was following close behind.

The clock had arrived so soon that it caught me off guard. It had been designed, built and delivered in just 11 days and I hadn't requested a bulletin board to go with it yet. So off I went to the Facilities department to put in my order in person. I explained to my Facilities contact (the same one that had given me the frosty brush-off on my first day on the job) that we needed an eight-foot bulletin board to post project status on.

"No problem," she said. "I'll have one for you in four weeks."

Eager to get the clock in action, I asked if we could speed up the process and was informed that "four weeks is the normal turnaround time for our vendor". Not to be put off easily, I asked for the phone number of the vendor to see if I could speed things up a bit and was told, "That's not your job."

Ouch. Another solid head butt from the Organizational Immune System™.

Back upstairs in Geoff's office it was my turn to do a little venting. Geoff had a good laugh over what had just happened and said, "Hey, go get the clock and we'll set it up here in my office for now. It will come in handy when I do some one-on-one meetings."

So that's what we did. We set up this giant digital clock in his office, then sat there and marveled at it like two giddy kids with a new toy.

The next adventure came with deciding where to mount the clock and the bulletin board. The R&D team was spread over several floors so we needed to pick someplace that would be visible to all 500 R&D'ers. Geoff proposed moving it around between floors but I didn't relish the task of enrolling Facilities in several clock moves. I suggested the entranceway to the cafeteria – after all, everybody had to eat, and it would be nice to give the entire company some exposure to what R&D was up to. Geoff agreed, but said that he would have to bounce the idea off the Senior

Management team at their next staff meeting. To my surprise, our CFO was next in line to give us a shot from the Organizational Immune System™.

The CFO was concerned that analysts and other company visitors could glean confidential insider information from the bulletin board about what products we had under development. Geoff and I agreed that his concern was more likely one of embarrassment should R&D continue the trend of running late on so many projects. Geoff, the determined diplomat, assured the CFO that we would remove all of the bulletin-board contents at any time, should he have important customers or investors on site.

It took us four weeks, but we got our bulletin board and we got the go-ahead to have the clock mounted outside the cafeteria entrance.

The day before the clock went up on the wall, Geoff called another Town Hall. There'd been a breakthrough: Ian Duncan, a long-time employee and regarded as one of the brightest engineering minds in the department, had found a way to make the mate-link problem go away. When the good news made its way to us, Ian was quick to caution that he had not fixed the problem – he had simply written a software routine that would make the mate-link error go away each time it occurred – the system was now "self-healing". This event was another that proved very telling about the culture and the way that people behaved: our engineers were chasing perfection over practicality. Whether the problem was gone or self-healing didn't matter to customers.

The news about the mate-link fix was good news. Even though the two-week deadline had long since passed, the R&D department now had an important win to crow about.

By this time many people had heard about the clock, and had stopped by Geoff's office to see it. We had it set up and running at the front of the room as Geoff spoke. On the big screen behind him he displayed the project management sheet showing how all of our projects were running late. Once again he explained to the assembled crowd the importance of "sense of urgency" and reiterated his "tyranny-of-the-OR-and-brilliance-of-the-AND" pitch. It was time to mind the seconds and not the months.

With the clock ensconced in the cafeteria hallway, we devoted the first bulletin board display to an explanation of what the clock was and how it worked. I'd spend part of my lunch hours making my pitch to anybody who stopped by and even so much as feigned interest. After a week, we posted the ten most important projects and their deliverable dates on the board. Morale was on an upswing. We had the mate-link issue behind us. The R&D team seemed to be enjoying their heightened profile across the company, provided by the news of the big clock in the hallway. Everything was going well.

Too well.

About three months after the clock went on public display, the first project deliverable on the bulletin board below came due. And then it passed unsuccessfully. I felt a little deflated as I looked at the bulletin board and innocently took out a red marker pen and placed a big red X across the posted deliverable date as a way of saying "date not achieved". An hour later the project status sheet of the errant project was ripped from the bulletin board, red X and all, and thrown on the project manager's desk. It was another defining moment and, as soon as he found out, Geoff was quick to act. A Town Hall was called for the next day and Geoff stood at the front of the room holding the project status sheet with the red X through the date. He told the assembled group what had happened. He told them he was disappointed that someone had tried to point a finger of blame at the project manager. He told them that if R&D wasn't ready to accept the embarrassment of missing a date, then we were fooling ourselves and simply removing the embarrassing red X didn't fix anything. We had already seen the evidence of our transparency on the Tucson Tape. He seized the opportunity to hammer home the fact that it was teamwork that got projects delivered on time (not finger-pointing when things went awry) and that we were all going to have to take it on the chin until we started delivering things on time.

Footnote: Our CFO became a supporter of the project clock and never once asked that the bulletin-board items be taken down. Part of this was because we used code names for all of our projects, as most high-tech companies do as a manner of prudent business practice. And secondly, I think he realized that things like the project clock were having an important impact on R&D, which was one of his largest areas of expenditure.

Geoff's Thoughts On This

I had my doubts about the clock being an effective tool to help instill a sense of urgency, but Steve was so excited about this idea and had been very creative in producing the Tucson Tape, so I deferred to him and let him proceed. However, my nagging doubts continued as he progressed through the company bureaucracy to get the clock ordered and installed. I think mainly it was because I saw the clock as being a negative – something people would want to avoid, rather than a positive motivator, like positive feedback.

Once the clock arrived and we put it in my office, I started to warm to the idea of having this big "countdown" and being able to point to it when meetings started to drag on and people were arguing for the sake of arguing and not getting back to business. But when Steve proposed putting the clock by the cafeteria with the projects list underneath, I wondered if we should be that public with our data. In the end, the clock provided another opportunity for me to emphasize that it was R&D, not Project Management, who was responsible for meeting delivery dates.

Later I learned that the clock was nicknamed the "Doomsday Clock" by the R&D engineers, referring to the movie "Dr. Strangelove", counting down the seconds to disaster. It reinforced my feeling that the clock was a negative motivator.

It was around this time that John Millard retired as CEO and Kirk Mandy was named as his replacement. Having a company insider promoted to CEO was good news for us. Kirk was fully aware of what we were doing in R&D so we didn't need to begin a campaign of educating a new person. To make the big changes we wanted to make we needed the support of the CEO, and we fully expected to have Kirk's support. He was well aware of the need to move from voice only to the world of converged voice and data.

Key Learnings

Company

- Whether a problem is gone or self-healing doesn't matter to customers.

- Scoreboards, with up-to-date metrics on important business goals work to motivate people.

Change Champion

- Look for things that motivate people in a positive way and gain benefits for the business at the same time. Avoidance of a negative consequence is less effective for people and the business in the long run.

Change Agent

- Find the source of leverage to motivate your clients. In this case it was pride, but the source of leverage will vary by situation.

- Pride, accomplishment, learning, and fear are all powerful motivators. Positive feelings like the feeling of accomplishment and pride will pay dividends by getting people to contribute more. Negative feelings like fear and shame will get compliance but nothing more.

- Give people lots to gain by achieving their goals. Emphasize the positives and celebrate every person or team that hits their target successfully.

CHAPTER 9

Sacred Cow Workshops: The Cow Patties Hit The Fan – Steve

GETTING READY FOR THE WORKSHOPS

Dr. Mike had been providing good advice throughout my first year on the job – challenging my thinking and providing great reading material. Now that Geoff and I had a few wins behind us and some defining moments had occurred, Dr. Mike was convinced it was time to ratchet things up a notch or two. He felt that we had the organization ready for movement but we needed more organizational shock therapy to help us move forward.

Among his many strengths Mike is an expert at the use of business simulations. Simulations are role-playing activities of specific situations in a mock work environment that participants pretend to be employed by for a couple of hours. The group then debriefs to discuss and measure their success. Many simulations offer the participants a chance to redesign the situation/factory/roles and run the exercise again to measure improvements.

I had used simulations before and was also a big fan of their use. I called them "deflection exercises". Simulations break down defensiveness by solving similar issues outside of the direct organizational context. If I take a group of people and put them in a room and say, "OK, folks, we've got some big problems and we've got to change the way we do things around here," I'll get a lot of "you-can't-possibly-be-talking-to-me" stares. I think that approach is a lot like asking people to perform surgery on themselves. By contrast, a good business simulation makes the situation neutral and the defensiveness falls away. When you debrief the simulation the participants will tell you all the things wrong with the simulated environment and engage in discussions about what they would do differently. Then you can quickly ease them into a discussion about "how our environment back at the office is just like this".

As I mulled over the idea of doing a business simulation with R&D, I reflected on the advice shared months ago by HR about the change workshop they ran. The feedback they had received was that the session was too light on content and not busy enough to justify the participants' time. I shared this with Dr. Mike as we began our prep work. Mike had a particular simulation in mind that he thought would work well with our highly technical department. It was a very detailed and complex simulation that ran for three hours with 700 pages of instructions and lots of problem-solving.

Mike was teaching in the Applied Social Sciences faculty at Concordia University in Montreal at that time and he had given his students the assignment of participating in a real-life project as part of their curriculum. I agreed to take on a group of students to help design a change workshop for our R&D department.

One late evening at the office, I gathered together all of my diagnostic data to date: Dr. Mike's "Around Here We Behave As If…" document, the Tucson Tape, the data from my original poster campaign, the angry letter from one of our customers to the CEO, the project management sheet, summaries of Geoff's rants, and my daily log book with notes about all the key interactions with HR and Facilities. I sat at my keyboard for a very long time into the evening and wrote a document called "The Culture Treatise of Mitel's R&D Department". I summarized my thoughts on why a "sense of urgency" was missing and why morale was low. The implementation plan of the Treatise called for a "culture-shock" workshop for all R&D employees as phase one, to be followed up by a formal leadership/business training program for all managers.

As I pondered this idea of "culture shock" to help instill a sense of urgency and boost morale, I put on my marketing hat and racked my brain for a talisman to summarize the problem. Mitel (like most high-tech organizations) had its own lexicon, which was so heavily laced with acronyms that an outsider would need a glossary to understand most conversations. Maybe our culture-shock session needed its own acronym and maybe what the organization needed was a form of CPR to revive it. Now what could CPR stand for? The C was easy – we had to *change*. The P was pretty easy too – we needed everyone in R&D to *participate* in the change (remember Geoff was willing to carry the wounded but not the stragglers). The R stood for *responsibility* – everyone had a responsibility to the company to help with the change.

I sent a copy of the Treatise and my jazzy CPR acronym off to Geoff and to Dr. Mike. Taking all 500 R&D employees off-site for the culture-shock workshop was going to be costly, so this was my first form of a pitch to Geoff. Mike came over to Mitel a couple of days later and together we made a more formal pitch to Geoff, with a rough outline that included the idea of using a simulation as the deflection exercise, and the rest of the time away to get the group involved in designing real changes to the way that things were currently being done. We also pitched the idea of a student group helping with the workshop design. Our outline called for a four-day workshop, off-site, with 100 R&D'ers at a time. Geoff was concerned about the length of the program and the cost for doing it off-site, but at least he did commit to us going ahead with a more detailed workshop design. The culture-shock workshop was alive for now.

The Concordia OD students – Charles, Chris, Camy and Lynn – began weekly meetings at Mitel.

After our first few weekly meetings, we had roughed out the agenda items for the culture-shock workshop:

- A complex simulation that highlighted accurate problem-solving, dissemination of complex communication, managing risk and quick decision-making;
- A debrief of the simulation that would lead into a discussion of things we needed to change;
- A brainstorm of our shortcomings and outdated practices;
- Breakout sessions for team members to rework policies, practices, and procedures affecting their group;
- Senior leader guest speakers from Mitel;

- A review of the company financials by CEO Kirk Mandy;
- A motivational speaker;
- A future visioning exercise.

I reread Ricardo Semler's book *Maverick*[5] as we prepared the culture-shock workshop. As Mike and I brainstormed themes for the workshop, the idea of "Sacred Cows" kept coming up in our conversations. A Sacred Cow is something in an organization that is rarely talked about yet is held in a kind of false respect and not openly criticized. Sacred Cows may be policies or patterns of behavior that people are reluctant to change because they have become comfortable with them over time. Sacred Cows are barriers to change and are symbolic of the Organizational Immune System™. We thought that if we could get the engineers talking in terms of these Sacred Cows, it might create a safety zone to examine all of our processes and policies.

The students liked the Sacred Cow idea too and we quickly got on a brainstorming roll. We could have an evening BBQ, record Sacred Cows on special "cow patties" and burn them at an evening bonfire and hand out cow paraphernalia for anyone caught killing a Sacred Cow. We wanted what seemed impossible:

- we wanted people to have fun while changing, and
- we wanted to make the change happen *with* people and not *at* them.

A week later Dr. Mike dropped by my office to deliver another book: *Sacred Cows Make the Best Burgers* by Robert Kriegel and David

Brandt.[6] From this moment of inspiration another idea was born. We bought 100 copies of both the *Sacred Cows* book and Semler's *Maverick* as pre-reading prep work to get everyone ready for the workshops. Each of the 100 workshop participants would have a choice to read either *Maverick* or *Sacred Cows Make the Best Burgers* before attending. After the workshop they would be required to return the books to our internal library where the next batch of workshop participants could access them. We now had a theme for the workshop that everyone could relate to.

The workshop design and preparations were coming along well, but I was still concerned about making a sizable enough impression on the participants and wracked my brain for some kind of significant emotional event to carry the day. The simulation that Mike had planned would be productive and fun, but our workshop still needed something visceral – akin to the impact of the Tucson Tape. I had a funny Dilbert cartoon on my bulletin board: Dilbert complains to Wally that his boss gave him a pink slip, and in the final frame Dilbert appears wearing a woman's pink slip.

What if we handed out pink slips?

That night when the design team came in for our weekly meeting I pitched them an idea. We would take the project management worksheet (the one that showed that every product was running late), photocopy it onto pink pieces of paper, and have Kirk hand one to everyone as the lead-in to his presentation for the financials. The student group was shocked by the idea and thought that it was too strong a symbolic message to give to the employees. They unanimously voted the idea down, fearing that valuable employees would flee the company. At that point I knew that it was a winner. We had already learned from the R&D

clock that pride was the most powerful motivating lever with this group, so a significant emotional event that highlighted our own shortcomings would be perfect.

With a little more digging through my diagnostics file, I dug out two more pieces of paper: a newspaper clipping from the financial section of a national newspaper slamming Mitel's overall company performance, and the angry email that a customer had written to then CEO John Millard. I carefully taped the project management sheet, the customer letter, and newspaper clipping to the front and back of a piece of paper and photocopied it onto pink paper as a prototype.

Geoff agreed that the "pink slips" would be a good wake-up call for the audience and he wasn't worried about scaring anybody away. On the other hand he wasn't entirely on board with my CPR acronym. He agreed with the "Change" and "Participation" but didn't like the idea of telling everyone that it was their "Responsibility" to get on board. He preferred the word "Leadership" – he wanted to inspire people in the department to step up to the challenge and help lead change rather than harp about their duty to the company. This was classic pull versus push strategy and I fully agreed. Of course CPL certainly didn't have the same cachet as CPR did, but Geoff was really warming up to the idea of running the workshop so I decided that this was not a hill to die on. Similarly, "culture-shock workshop" was dropped from our vocabulary and the session was officially dubbed the "CPL workshop".

Geoff told me that he had sent a copy of the Culture Treatise to CEO Kirk Mandy, and that Kirk had read it. Geoff encouraged me to meet with Kirk and get his insight on the situation as we continued the final workshop design. We were going to need Kirk's support both on the funding for the sessions and as one of the key guest speakers.

The meeting with Kirk went better than I expected. He agreed that R&D was missing a sense of urgency, and he thought that the reason was that the department had "lost their confidence". When I asked him about funding the workshop he said, "Hey, you guys have a budget and if this is how you plan to spend it then that is your choice." I knew that I had just been handed some rope – you can either cut yourself some slack or you can hang yourself with it. I didn't miss the unspoken warning in Kirk's message: this was going to be an expensive investment so it better be a good use of the money. To my surprise, Kirk immediately agreed to be a guest speaker and agreed to give everyone some insight into the company's financial status.

In the car on the way home that night I put on my marketing hat and made a cell phone call to Gary Frederick – a local artist who has a special talent for being able to take my verbal descriptions and turn them into artistic representations. I explained to Gary that we were about to do a Sacred Cow hunt and that we'd need a cool T-shirt logo (never underestimate the power of a simple T-shirt to help promote your product). I wanted a chef flipping burgers in the background with a worried looking cow in the foreground. By the time I returned to work the next morning the drawing was on the fax machine waiting for me. Having a network of talented people like Gary was invaluable when it came to turning ideas into action at short notice.

Artwork by Gary Frederick—gdfpro.com

Over the next couple of weeks our workshop design team continued to hone the agenda, assemble a workbook, prepare slideshows, print T-shirts, and put together a list of guest speakers in preparation for the CPL workshops. Geoff had been busy too, and had hired a new director of Software Design, which eased the day-to-day load on him.

Geoff committed to a trial run of the CPL workshop with a smaller audience of 40 – all of his direct reports and a cross-section of R&D managers. He balked at the four-day agenda and instructed us to cut it down to three days. With the "work 'em hard" advice from the HR team still in my head we decided to keep the amount of content intact and just work longer days. At the back of my mind I was concerned that Geoff was only going to buy into doing the workshop with this one group of R&D managers. I knew that we need to put every R&D employee through the workshop and began thinking about what it was going to take to sway him. This was going to be expensive and it was going to cost the entire R&D organization three days of productivity, but I was convinced that it was necessary for everyone to experience it. Just like getting an unfiltered voice of customer message was important, giving everyone exposure to the CPL workshop was necessary for its success.

When it came time to pick a location, Geoff lobbied to hold the session at the Chateau Montebello – a historic retreat hotel in Quebec that has been host to the rich, famous and powerful over the years. People like Winston Churchill, Pierre Trudeau, Margaret Thatcher, Ronald Reagan, Bing Crosby and Joan Crawford have been guests of the hotel. I was concerned about the location. First of all it was set up for weddings and conferences, not for the type of workshop that we were about to roll out. Secondly, I didn't want the workshop to have the reputation as a boondoggle at a luxury resort. I had located a professional training campus in Cornwall – about two hours in the opposite direction from the Chateau Montebello – which was set up for large-scale training events. It was complete with small dorm rooms, theatre hall and cafeteria, and would welcome us for a small fraction of the cost of Montebello. Cornwall had nothing that smacked of retreat; it had an overwhelming feel of university for grown-ups. Geoff dug his heels in for Montebello and again, it wasn't a hill worth dying on, so Dr. Mike and I decided that we would just have to make the best of it. My concern about Geoff just wanting to do this for the managers strengthened. We really needed to impress him with this workshop. The hotel could accommodate us the following Wednesday through Friday so we booked it and geared up for the first session.

Managers and Cows at the Chateau

To keep people from straying away from the hotel at night we bussed them there, leaving their cars at the office. The buses left Mitel at 7:00 a.m. – an ungodly early hour for a high-tech crowd and a move that won us no favors. Once seated in a hotel conference room by 9:00 a.m., Geoff opened the session by asking the assembled group of managers a list of questions that was printed on the first page of their workbooks:

1. What are the hallmarks of R&D?

2. Who is the most important person to Mitel?

3. What is our targeted Return on Sales?

4. Who is the enemy?

5. Who are our main competitors in the industry?

6. Who can help us win in the marketplace?

He got very few correct answers, and told the group that we were going to begin each day with this list of questions and that by the end of day three they would all have the right answers. He also called everyone's attention to another page close to the front of the workbook. On this page everyone was going to record two things that they were going to do differently. The heading read, "On Monday, I am going to begin to implement my action plan by…". Geoff informed everyone that they were going to be called upon to stand in front of the group and read these two items aloud at the workshop closing ceremonies. The message was clear – we are not here to play, we're here to work. The message was the same as the project clock: for the organization to be successful, people will be held accountable for doing what is asked of them.

I was up next. On top of scheduling the early start to the day, I further angered the crowd by administering a comprehension test on their homework. Had they indeed read one of the two books assigned as pre-reading? By the immediate angry reaction to the test I knew that some of them had not done their homework and we were once again hurting their pride with the prospect of finding them out. People wanted to know why we were treating them like children. Didn't we trust them? Geoff was quick to wade into the foray and told the group that starting today everyone was going to be held accountable for their actions. If they had indeed done what we had asked them then they were just being held accountable and there was nothing to fear. In the end we did not mark the "tests" or even collect them, we simply took up the answers in an open forum. We had accomplished what we intended to do – we called their bluff at not doing their homework.

The simulation that Dr. Mike had chosen worked like magic. Despite the three-hour hard deadline given to the teams for round one, they debated issues and frittered away valuable time. By noon, as round one was shut down, many of the teams were quite dejected by their failures until they realized that *all* teams failed to accomplish a successful end to the simulation. After lunch the teams were sent off to begin their redesign work. Later that evening, Geoff, Dr. Mike and myself formed a panel that held court to the redesign teams. One by one the teams came up and described what had gone wrong, what they had learned, and what their strategy was going to be for round two. The teams got into the spirit of adventure, and the presentations were really funny. Since I had angered the group twice at the front end of the session, I was particularly relieved to see that they had regained their sense of humor.

The new director of Software Design spent his third day on the job at the workshop, and he was meeting many of his new team for the first time. The session turned out to be a great orientation for him. The presentations continued until after 11:00 p.m. We had been going for 16 hours when we brought the day to a close and announced that the second run of the simulation would begin at 8:30 the next morning. We had anticipated an earlier end to the evening and arranged for an open bar, so after the redesign presentations the beer began to flow.

Mike and I were both concerned about a prompt start to day two, but much to our surprise teams began arriving early to set up for the second round of the sim. Once again Geoff opened the workshop with his list of questions from page one of their workbook. By the beginning of day two, they learned a few more of the answers.

When round two of the simulation was called to a close just before lunch, all teams but one had met with success. Ironically it was the team that endured a second loss that became the biggest advocate for change throughout the rest of the workshop. They had suffered the embarrassment of two losses and once again, pride had been hurt. It was one thing to fail round one along with everyone else, but suffering another loss in round two (with the benefit of learning from round one) was almost too much for them to bear. They were determined not to be caught as laggards again. The debrief for this simulation was just as we imagined. People got the connection between the ills of the simulated environment and our actual work environment. The light bulbs went on, and they realized how our own organizational pitfalls were not being addressed.

Engineering Cracks the Code

The simulation that we selected for the Sacred Cow workshops turned out to be perfect for an engineering organization. It was a very detailed simulation centered around accurate problem-solving, dissemination of complex communication and managing risk. It had over 700 pages of instructions that flooded out to the teams over the three hour run time. One of the decisions that each team needed to make was whether or not to buy a special decoder device. Some of the messages flowing to the teams were encrypted. If they opted to purchase the decoder (actually a square tube constructed from Lego blocks), a communications expert (one of the facilitators) would exchange their encrypted message for a message in plain text. Some of the messages that were encrypted were important and others were not.

The second group to attend a workshop did something that we didn't anticipate. The garbled or encrypted messages were actually created using a fairly low level of computer code. One group, instead of buying the decoder to unscramble their messages, devoted time finding an algorithm to unscramble the code. Two people on their team spent a lot of the three-hour simulation time on it and did manage to crack the code. On the one hand we were astonished that they would waste the time doing this and on the other hand we were amazed that they were able to do it.

Needless to say, this group failed at the first run of the simulation despite their best sleuthing efforts. Their debrief was meaningful because they realized that they had got too far down into the weeds of details and lost sight of the larger picture of what their task was.

- Steve

After lunch, Kirk arrived on time and handed out sealed envelopes before starting his financial presentation. As he walked through the audience handing out the envelopes he quipped, "Don't open your pink slips yet," which generated nervous laughter. Once back at the podium, he invited everyone to open his or her envelope. As soon as the color pink surfaced, the room got really quiet as he told them to read the sheet carefully. After letting this group of R&D managers sit in silence for a few minutes, Kirk did a masterful job on the pink slips and turned the situation around 180 degrees.

He said, "Look, I'm not giving anyone a pink slip. I need each and every one of you. We're not overstaffed and we're not about to do any layoffs. But just read those sheets. We are giving ourselves pink slips! If you think that the way we are performing is a secret from anyone you are wrong. We have customers who hate us. Financial analysts are writing nasty things in the national papers about us. And what are we doing? We're letting every project run late."

He didn't say anything more about the pink slips, and just launched into an explanation of our current financial situation. Where we were making money, where we were investing (and not making money yet), and where we were not making money. Kirk explained how Quality issues and missed opportunities due to slow product releases were hurting our bottom line. The big shock factor that Kirk delivered was that the profitability of the Systems division was a paltry one half percent. To put this in context, for every $100 of Mitel telephone systems sold, we kept only 50 cents as profit. Product support costs (resulting from poor Quality), and a weak revenue stream from new software features, were killing us.

In the Company of Sacred Cows

The Q&A session that followed was really good, and Kirk killed off a few Sacred Cows himself as he fielded questions about marketing expenses, executive salaries, and other perks.

Dr. Mike was up next, and he engaged the audience in an open discussion about change. Like a maestro conducting an orchestra, he pulled out slides on change theory and translated them into everyday examples.

After Mike's session I presented a slideshow. It was a light-hearted look at customer service situations, starting with a picture of the business wicket at a bank that had a sign saying, "We do not accept cash". (I almost got arrested for using a camera inside a bank.) It continued with photos of things that frustrate consumers in retail stores. Everyone was getting a good chuckle out of the slides and then we came to the photos of our office. I had taken a bunch of early-morning pictures at the office: messy workstations piled high with equipment, parts, and junk. The photographs didn't speak of an efficient and effective high-tech company – in their quiet simplicity they spoke of an organization in disarray and decay. Once again the audience got quiet, and as they sat there in the dark, looking at the pictures projected on the screen, you could see light bulbs going on in their heads.

By 10:00 p.m. on day two of the workshop we were still going strong when our motivational speaker took the stage. Dr. Sharon Rolbin focused in on this group of managers and gave them their marching orders. "You only have three tasks," she told them: "Give your employees the tools to do their jobs, put a fire in their bellies, and then get out of the way." Geoff and I both nodded in agreement – this is exactly what we were trying to do with this group.

As Sharon finished, Kirk made his way to the front of the room to make a quick announcement. He wanted the managers to be the first to know that Mitel had just purchased Gandalf – another local high-tech company. Cheers went up from the audience. For the first time in many years Mitel was showing signs of strength – we were now a company on the hunt for acquisitions.

By midnight Dr. Mike and I were standing by the bar fielding follow-up questions about the day. Despite two back-to-back 16-hour days (and many had stayed up until the wee hours of day one) nobody seemed tired. There was a real buzz in the air. We were getting through to them.

At the close of the session on the afternoon of day three, the long days and emotional high had taken its toll on the group. They were jazzed but drained. One important task still stood between us and the end of day. It was time for everyone to stand and read their two things that they were going to change starting Monday morning. Getting every participant to stand and make this kind of commitment was going to be the true test of how successful the workshop had been. Would people suggest things that others needed to change? Would they come up with trivial things? Geoff surprised me, and the entire room, by going first. He told the group that he wasn't just here as a facilitator of the workshop but as a participant too, and with that he read the two change items that he had written in his workbook.

First, Geoff was going to move his office to another floor. We had spent a lot of time discussing communication, and Geoff told the managers that he was going to move to give employees easier "drop-in" access to him. (As a footnote, Geoff continued to move his office about every nine months thereafter.) Secondly, he announced that on Monday morning he was going to sign several blank travel authorization forms. Many employees had identified the inability to travel as a Sacred Cow. "How could they go out and get the voice of the customer themselves on important issues when it was so hard to get travel authorized?" Of course the tight reins on travel were a holdover from the ultra-conservative days under BT. After Geoff finished, people took turns one at a time reading their action items for change. I crossed my fingers and prayed that their enthusiasm would carry through to next Monday morning.

Two days later I got my answer. Teams were shocked by the behavior of the managers who had been away at Montebello. Managers were going around changing things – abandoning useless policies, delegating tasks, holding people accountable, praising those who were exhibiting the right behaviors, rearranging schedules so that employees could be away for three days of training themselves and, of course, ensuring that their employees were reading one of the two prescribed books.

The Cows Move to Cornwall

Mid-week, Dr. Mike, Geoff and I gathered to debrief the first "Sacred Cow workshop", as they were now known. By this time, I had Geoff's full support for putting the entire R&D organization through them. It was just a matter of timing, refinements, and budget. We unanimously decided that the sessions needed to continue to run on a Wednesday-to-Friday schedule. At the end of the workshop, everyone was mentally and physically exhausted and needed a weekend's worth of sleep before returning to the office. On average, workshop participants would log 40 hours of work time over the three days at CPL. A bit of down-time also gave participants a chance to reflect on their Sacred Cows and let the workshop learnings sink in before returning to the office. For our part, we decided on a few changes: Kirk's pink slip envelopes would have even greater impact if each one was individually addressed to workshop participants; adding a fun movie to the evening of day two; inviting a customer to each session as a guest speaker; expanding the workshop to include 100 participants at a time, and theme uniforms for Geoff, Mike, and me as the facilitators of the simulation. We also agreed that the round of beer at the end of each day was valuable time for the participants to do their own debrief and connect the dots, so to speak.

I also wanted to change the venue away from Montebello to Cornwall where the facilities were better equipped for this type of session and much better priced. Rather than raise the issue at this meeting, I just went ahead and booked Cornwall and informed Geoff about it few days before the session date. I figured it was time to really stick my neck out and hoped that the road to forgiveness was easier than the road to permission. I got lucky on this one.

One workshop exercise called for participants to write down as many Sacred Cows as they could, and read some of the best ones aloud to the group. I thought it would be even more fun to post these Cows up somewhere so I went to a local lumberyard and bought a big sheet of plywood. In my garage I cut out a life-sized cow and painted "Bessie" white with black spots. Bessie appeared at all future workshops and became our bulletin board for collecting Sacred Cows. When workshop participants arrived back at the office on Monday mornings, Bessie was set up in the foyer to greet each of them and remind them that they had two particular to-do items for their first day back. As a footnote: by the time we had completed all five workshops, the Sacred Cows notes posted on Bessie filled a 72-page website.

Sprinkler Cow

People were really having a lot of fun with the cow theme and cow paraphernalia kept showing up in my office. At one point someone had returned from a weekend shopping venture at the local flea market and brought me a plastic cow that had a tail made of flexible tubing with a lawn sprinkler attached to it. When attached to a garden hose, the tail of the cow swayed back and forth powered by the spray of the sprinkler on the other end.

We already had Bessie the Sacred Cow bulletin board as an official greeter in the foyer every Monday following a workshop so I thought it might be fun to have the sprinkler cow outside the building too. Arriving at work early on a Monday morning with the plastic cow and my garden hose from home I went to see the maintenance people in Facilities.

They gave me the special key needed to turn on water to the outside taps and away I went. Within a couple of minutes I had the cow nicely set up on the front lawn, the garden hose attached and the water flowing. It was quite a sight!

Around 9:30 I went back down to turn the water off and remove sprinkler cow. When I got outside it was gone. No sight of it at all. Hmmmmm. Back inside to visit with the Director of Facilities I was chastised for disregarding the "corporate standard for watering the lawn". Gordon was really intent upon knowing where I had got the key to open the water tap. Not wanting to get my helpful maintenance fellow in any trouble I held out on releasing the information. Similarly Gordon held out on telling me where the plastic cow and my hose were.

On my way out of the Facilities department I swung by the maintenance workshop to quietly return the water key to my friend. I assured him that he *had done no wrong and that knowledge of where the key had came from was safe. He in turn hinted at the back area of the shop where I could find the plastic cow and hose.*

Despite all of our progress in getting rid of Sacred Cows in R&D, they were still clearly grazing in other departments.

- Steve

The rest of the workshops followed the same pattern. The tweaks that we introduced after the first session cemented a truly great agenda. Kirk juggled his schedule to make it to the workshops to deliver his "pink-slip" talk. We personalized every envelope, so now it was no longer generic – it had your name on it. The pink slips were collected at the end of every session and participants sworn to secrecy so that those coming next could get the full effect of this exercise. The simulation, guest speakers, movies and slideshow always had the same powerful effect. On Friday afternoon the participants would stand and read their commitment to change, and at every workshop Geoff too would stand and add to his list of Cows that he was going to kill. The following Monday back at the office – BAM! – 200 things would change. Before long, the R&D department was no longer seen as the black sheep of the company. Managers from other departments were phoning my office asking, "What the heck are you guys doing down there in Cornwall? People come back really different." Employees from other departments were asking for invitations to the workshop (or encouraging their managers to go sign up). We never turned anyone away.

Even Geoff was impressed by the Cornwall facility and the learning atmosphere there. I was pleased with the facility too – it was a lot more cost effective than a luxury chateau and I was now running well below my projected budget. I'd go to Cornwall on the Tuesday night before each session with Bessie and all of the other workshop materials in the back of a pickup truck. After checking in I'd go to the local beer store and stock up on large quantities of beer for the hospitality suite so that we wouldn't have to pay bar prices. Geoff would often come along to help slug the cases of beer into the coolers. It was about 3:00 a.m. on the first night that we hosted 100 employees in Cornwall when Geoff came up to me and said excitedly, "It's 3:00 a.m. and they're still all talking about work!" I think those evening sessions were the best part of the workshops. All day long we'd light the fire for change and every evening employees would talk about ways to make it real. The Sacred Cow workshops were work hard / play hard events.

Geoff had heard from many engineers that "over at Newbridge you could have a beer after 5:00 p.m." and was challenged by R&D to do the same.

Geoff wanted to keep the idea of "shop talk over a beer" alive beyond Sacred Cow sessions so he tackled another big Sacred Cow with the executive team.

At Mitel there was a moratorium against any kind of alcohol in the building. Anyone who brought in alcohol faced likely termination. On top of all this, our company lawyer was up in arms about liability issues with drinking and driving. Once again Geoff persevered and assured the Senior Management team that they were dealing with responsible adults and offered his personal guarantee that he would monitor consumption. With another Sacred Cow gone, the R&D department started a ritual of the Friday "R&D Social" beer after work. We always held the shop-talk sessions in a large R&D conference room. At the end of every session the whiteboards were full of squiggly electrical diagrams and partial algorithms. We never had problems with consumption; a lot of problems got solved in those two hours at the end of every week.

Geoff's Thoughts On This:

I admit that I originally had questions about the workshop. I wondered whether or not it was necessary, but after everyone had been through this process they came back to the company with a definite commitment to Quality and a commitment to developing new IP products.

I got tested at the workshops a number of times as I would talk about Quality, Time-To-Market, and killing Sacred Cows. One of our engineers, Paul, joked at one session, "Well, you know, if I had a bed at Mitel, I could spend more time there, therefore I'd get more done and the Time-To-Market would decrease because I'd be working more hours." Everyone thought that was pretty funny and I wasn't sure if he was just joking or poking fun at us. I didn't say anything at the time, but the next week after everyone came back to work, Steve and I went down to Sears and bought one of those rollaway cots. We put it in the elevator, took it up to the sixth floor, rolled it right into his cubicle, and I said, "Here you go; you asked for it, I'm delivering. So I expect you to keep up your end of the bargain and reduce Time-To-Market." It only cost me $150 and it made quite a statement inside the organization: "Be careful what you ask for!"

The other thing I was challenged on during the Sacred Cow workshops was travel. If R&D people wanted to visit a customer, they felt that they would have trouble doing so because of the bureaucracy of going through umpteen levels of management to get a travel requisition signed. At the meeting I committed to pre-approve some travel requisitions and leave them on file with my assistant. Any R&D person could see Nancy, tell her where they were going, who they were going to see and why; she would hand over the travel req and they'd be on their way. There was a hush over the crowd.

I learned that you're going to be tested on how committed you are as a leader to making things happen. That's exactly what happened to me. None of those travel reqs were ever used. The Sacred Cow was not the travel req process itself, but the perception that employees were not allowed to go and visit customers themselves. I killed that Cow.

As a result of the workshop people began looking at things differently, questioning why we continued to do things the way we did, and that was all very good.

Key Learnings

Company

- The organization change process has to touch everyone to be most effective.

Change Champion

- Once you walk the talk, you need to get your direct reports walking the talk as well. After a couple of layers of the hierarchy get aligned, there's a cascading effect and the rest of the organization falls more readily into line.

Change Agent

- Be prepared to fight to protect the essence of your cause, but be flexible and let others make it their own too. Ownership creates buy-in.

- To have the most impact, a large-scale change intervention needs the full support and co-facilitation of company leaders who have a vested interest in the outcome.

CHAPTER 10

The Day We Touched The Moon – Steve

ABOUT A MONTH after the last Sacred Cow workshop, Brian came into a staff meeting with an announcement. His Technical Support team had been working on an algorithm to measure the size of our Quality problem. Dubbed the Customer Dissatisfaction Index (or CDI for short) the algorithm measured three things:

- Bug severity (on a scale of 1 to 10). The Tech Support team developed a 10-point scale to determine how severe a bug was with 1 being a low (maybe the system reset itself every leap year) to 10 being high (random fault causing system to go off-line several times per day).

- Length of time since the bug had been first noticed (days). Our Tech Support call centre logged every bug that was reported by date, system type, configuration and customer name as soon as it came in.

- The number of systems sold that are likely to be affected by the bug. The team hypothesized that if a customer phoned in with a software bug then it was likely that all similar systems had the same bug and that either the customer hadn't called in to report it yet or the customer had not used that part of the software yet and the bug was still lying dormant. Either way, they wanted to be proactive and eliminate the problem for the customer whether it was reported or not.

For each bug, we performed this calculation:

Bug Severity * Length of time known * Number of systems sold.

The total CDI was the sum of all these calculations. When the math was done on that particular day, our measure of customer pain totaled 685,000. Brian and his team had found an indisputable way to measure and track one of our biggest issues – Quality. Eureka. Just as the project clock gave us a scoreboard to measure Time-To-Market, the Customer Dissatisfaction Index gave us a scoreboard to measure Quality.

Now the question begged: what was the right number? We all agreed that 685,000 was too high, but at the same time, an R&D organization that was constantly developing and releasing new products couldn't expect the number to be zero either. We were going to have to temper perfection with realism.

Geoff gave the team a few moments to discuss what they thought the right number should be. Stunned into silence, no one wanted to volunteer a number. Suggest something too high and you would look like a goldbricker in front of the boss, but by suggesting something too low you would be committing to a hefty challenge that could now be measured. After a few moments of awkward silence, Geoff announced, "If nobody's going to volunteer anything, I have a number in mind." Everyone cringed as he said "10,000" and another BHAG was born.

I wasn't sure where he came up with the number, but Geoff later told me that part of his management style was to always ask his team for their ideas on any decision – but at the same time to always have a ready answer in his own head in case nobody spoke up. This way nothing important was ever opened for discussion without a guaranteed outcome. If the team could come up with a good decision then all was well. If they couldn't, then he was ready to make the decision for them. On that day, a few brave souls attempted to refute the 10,000 threshold, but when pressed for their rationale, there was nothing to say whether 10,000 was either a good number or a bad number. We all recognized that it was a quantum leap from where we were at that moment and Geoff stood fast in his decision.

Another Town Hall was organized – this time to educate everyone on the new algorithm, and to keep the focus on Quality, making it everyone's responsibility. Unlike the mate-link issue, there would be no carrot for cracking the 10,000 CDI mark. This was the new status quo and the entire team had to figure out how to make it so.

At the end of this Town Hall there were a few questions. Where did the algorithm come from? Had we benchmarked this with other software development organizations? Where did the 10,000 figure come from? Geoff took the last question squarely on the chin. He had asked his management team to come up with a number and when they didn't, he picked 10,000. There was no science in it, but it wouldn't be reopened for discussion until they first took a shot at it. Following up with my engineering buddies after the Town Hall, there were the same mixed reactions that we had got at the mate-link Town Hall. The R&D department was hearing the Quality issue, and starting to take action, but the size of the task seemed daunting.

Brian kept the pressure on his Tech Support team and they looked for ways to break the rules too. The bug-fix process was ripe for some fresh thinking. Every bug that was logged into the system was recorded and tracked. Each one was worked on in due course. The problem was that due course meant that each bug was worked on and fixed before the next one was looked at, because this is the way they had always done it and somewhere along the line it became accepted as a rule that problems had to be solved in the order in which they were discovered. With the new challenge of driving the CDI below 10,000, the Tech Support team looked for opportunities to bring the number down in big chunks. The "first-in, first-served" system was challenged and soon declared to be a Sacred Cow; there was in fact no rule that said the bugs had to be solved in sequential order. With this Cow killed off, the techs began diving into the database and looking for bugs with big CDI scores associated with them. This allowed the bugs with the highest CDI scores, the ones with the most field impact, to be fixed first. The R&D people loved this system because it took the subjectiveness out of the process, and reassured them that fixing a bug with a high CDI score would have the most positive impact on customers. Once again they were challenging rules for all the right reasons. Bugs with small CDI numbers that didn't really affect customers were thrown out completely.

A graph was set up, and a schedule of weekly CDI reviews established. Every week, Tech Support teams came to the manager's office to report their number for that week and their estimate of their number for the following week. Each week, the CDI score was calculated and plotted on a graph in the hallway. Each week, people gathered around the graph to see the score. CDI was dropping fast.

It took them only nine months (mind you, it was still nine months of hard work), but in that time the team did the unthinkable. The CDI number dropped below the 10,000 mark. On one of our flagship products, the SX-200, the CDI even dropped to zero for a day. The SX-200 team still refers to this as the day they touched the moon.

The afternoon following, we had a celebration with a big cake and lots of smiles all around. We had turned another corner. R&D was having successes.

Geoff's Thoughts On This

One of the biggest questions in terms of bug-fixing is, "Which ones do you fix first?" Everyone has an opinion on the most severe and the most disruptive. Some people want all the bugs fixed before ever shipping a product, others are more cavalier. What works best for engineers is a quantifiable model, one that can be used to prioritize the bugs in an objective way. This is what the CDI accomplished. It provided a method of prioritizing bugs in the eyes of the customer: not R&D, not Sales, but in the eyes of the people using our systems. It was a tool that became the "thermometer" of Quality.

I found it quite surprising that when it came to picking a number to represent customer Quality, no one could suggest one. With the CDI so high, I would have thought someone would have suggested a high number. When I picked 10,000, I had no idea whether it could be reached or not. However, I did know that without a target to aim at we would flounder, and progress would be slow.

Key Learnings

Company

- Goals and targets give you something to aim for and foster organizational alignment.

- Goals need to be measurable and simple to understand.

- Goals need to reflect the company's purpose.

Change Champion

- Let people develop their own targets. If they can't or won't, be prepared to set them. Keep targets visible and talk about them.

- Sense of achievement is a more powerful and lasting motivator than monetary or tangible rewards.

Change Agent

- We are all creatures of measurement. People need to know the score. Make measurements visible and understood.

- Use interrelated targets (like fast and good) to keep balance (i.e. you can't rob Peter to pay Paul – you have to pay them both).

- Measures can be very rewarding or very punishing, so it's important to choose them carefully. Ideally, measures should be positive (like the CDI) rather than negative reinforcement (like the clock).

Chapter 11

Demo Day – Steve

BY THIS TIME, we felt that employees were moving beyond awareness of the changes that we needed to make and into action. Now was the time to build momentum and get the culture moved forward as far as possible. One issue that came up time and time again, from my initial poster campaign in the elevator lobby to the Sacred Cow sessions, was the difficulty of information-sharing across such a large department. Although the Friday Socials had made some progress on this front, we still had communication gaps across R&D. I often said that having R&D spread across three different floors in the building was akin to being on three different planets – these engineers rarely interacted with others outside of mandatory meetings or aside from their small cliques for lunch and coffee. I remembered a friend telling me about a similar problem at Industry Canada – one of our Federal Trade Ministries. They had tackled their internal information-sharing issue by holding an internal trade show once a year. With this in mind, I plotted "Demo Day" for R&D.

Demo Day was to be a glorified show-and-tell day, where every project team would put together a little display or presentation about what they were working on. Presentations and displays were to be done in the actual workspace of each project team – the theory being that if you wanted to follow up with someone the next day or next week, you would know where to find them. Each team was to be divided in two: the first half would be presenters for the morning, while the second half could walk about the floors and take in other demos. In the afternoon, team members would switch roles.

Geoff liked the idea, so we pitched it to the R&D leadership team at a staff meeting. We selected a date, and asked all the R&D managers to encourage their project teams to participate. We would open the day with a short Town Hall by Geoff, and close the day with a networking celebration, complete with a special guest speaker and prizes for the best demos. Over the next two weeks, we compiled a list of displays and presentations (along with their locations) and everyone assured me that the project teams would participate. But when I left the office at 6:00 p.m. on the night before Demo Day, my heart sank, as I saw very little activity to indicate anyone was setting up a display.

Returning to the office at 7:00 a.m. the next day, I got off the elevator and stopped dead in my tracks. It was as though Santa Claus had visited our office in the night. Everywhere I looked I saw signs, posters, computer displays, and the blinking LED lights of prototype hardware components. This was going to be a good day.

Geoff hosted the morning Town Hall, and welcomed everyone to our first annual Demo Day. He encouraged everyone to make the best of the day, and gave strict orders that no work was to be done. Today was for learning. He also announced that in addition to the prizes for the best demos, those who received the most checkmarks for visiting certain specific demos would be eligible for a special draw at the end of the day. This was his way of directing the organization to certain areas where collaboration could help reduce Time-To-Market issues.

The effect of Demo Day was fantastic, and pride showed through as project team members talked glowingly about their work. Our graphics artist, Chris, was my "go-to person" for internal communications. She had prepared for the day by making a bunch of buttons that proclaimed, "I'm an R&D Geek and proud of it." In the morning, only a few brave souls were wearing their buttons; by afternoon, most were wearing them. It was fun to watch teams putting up makeshift signage throughout the day to draw more traffic into their areas. Teams found people working on problems in one area that had already been solved in another. They found synergistic project elements that would speed up delivery times for both. They made new contacts within the department itself and made connections that otherwise would never have been made.

Geoff was working his magic throughout the day as well. He went over to the executive suites and gathered up his peers to come to Demo Day. Employees were really excited to see the President and the VPs wandering the floors, taking in the demos, and giving positive feedback to project teams. Sales and marketing team members not only got a firsthand view of the breadth of projects underway, but they also got to see the first version of the new VoIP product. The engineers had done it — they had managed to get an early version of the product up and running to showcase for this event, and they got the chance to demo it directly to the executives.

The Introvert/Extrovert Architecture for VoIP:

We needed a new product and, in particular, a new architecture for VoIP. At the time, we had two very strong individuals working on the design and they had different views as to what architecture would work best. Not only that, they had completely different personality styles.

Kim was very good thinking on his feet, answering questions and sounding convincingly like he had thought a particular issue through, when in actual fact he was sometimes "thinking out loud" as he went along. Debbie, being more of an introverted thinker, would spend two days and evenings working out her architecture in detail, as well as the approach to her actual presentation. But when questioned, specifically by Kim – who didn't think it was the right architecture and would argue with her – Debbie needed time to go away and think about her responses.

At first it looked like Kim had it well thought through and Debbie didn't; that there were "holes" in Debbie's architecture. And this created an antagonistic dynamic between the two of them and it would sometimes get quite personal, which was extremely upsetting to both, and to everyone in the room.

After a couple of times when Debbie came back a day or so later with very good reasons why there were no "holes", I clued in. So we established a new approach to critiquing: not making decisions right on the spot, but instead allowing time for everyone involved to go away and think about the proposed designs.

In the end, the approach we used was a combination of Kim's and Debbie's architectures. But it wasn't until I realized the importance of personality styles that this important and cooperative work got done.

- Geoff

Demo Day – Steve

At 4:00, everyone gathered downstairs for munchies and beer. The prizes were given out and we introduced our special guest speaker. I had hired comedian Johnny Wing to do 15 minutes of stand-up comedy to end the day with a few laughs. The show was going great and I could tell that Johnny wanted to end with a really big laugh and just couldn't get it to happen. As he worked the crowd to get the last laugh, his humor was quickly getting less appropriate and I saw my career flash before my eyes. Geoff told me later that a few of his fellow executives were laughing hysterically at the jokes and teasing him, "Hey, when you get fired over this we want your office furniture." I was just about to give Johnny the hook when he got his big finish and said goodnight. Nobody complained about Johnny, and the day went down in company history as another milestone of success for R&D.

Geoff's Thoughts On This:

Demo Day really helped to improve communication in R&D and it increased idea-sharing in the Software Design area in particular. One of the things we wanted to address in terms of decreasing Time-To-Market was reducing development time by sharing software. Object-oriented programming methods are supposed to help accomplish this – but if you don't know where the programs or subroutines or pieces are that you need, you'll just develop them yourself.

Demo Day was our way of getting people in the organization to see things we wanted them to see. It worked really well. People really enjoyed it because when you have your head down, you don't really have an opportunity to see people who are working on things that might be of use to you.

It was great to be able to showcase all of the good things going on in R&D to my peers. The employees were really excited to be able to demo their products to the senior team.

However, in retrospect, showing the other VPs the demo of the new VoIP product should have been a trigger for them to start reskilling their own organizations, to gear up for the product's delivery down the road. But it wasn't. Within my peer group of VPs I had been getting consistently positive feedback from everybody for getting the Quality problems fixed. But when it came to support for the new IP product that we were building, something odd was happening. My peers would support me in private, but when they were talking to their people or even customers, they wouldn't show the same level of commitment to the IP product development. I was the corporate spokesperson for VoIP, and I should have realized that, although flattering to me, this role really belonged the Head of Product Management or Marketing. We had a real disconnect on this issue that I should have recognized as a major red flag.

Key Learnings

Company

- With organizational size comes communication gaps. Being on different floors or in different cities can be communication killers.

- Meaningful internal communication is more than a "nice-to-do". It helps with the sharing of ideas, and eliminates redundant work.

Change Champion

- Be a witness to the everyday successes of your people.

- Be a conduit for your peers to be a witness to the successes of your people.

- Don't be afraid to poke your nose into the business of other departments to be sure that you are all aligned.

Change Agent

- Finding a simple, effective, and meaningful way for people to brag about themselves is a win-win for all. Look for the key events or interventions that will give you a quantum leap in internal communication.

Chapter 12

The Power Of Positive Feedback – Geoff

WHAT I LEARNED through Steve was how powerful and important recognition can be to changing behaviors. As an executive, I was always very busy, and during the period before I hired new directors of Hardware and Software Design, I was doing two jobs. R&D had the largest budget of any department in the company, so was under a lot of scrutiny – managing this budget took a lot of time.

At first Steve would come into my office and say things like, "You know, so-and-so has just taken two weeks out of the delivery cycle by coming up with an electronic way of releasing products into the factory. You should go congratulate him and recognize it right now because he just did this."

And I'd say, "Well, I'm busy, I'm doing things, I know it's a good thing to do but I'll do it later."

But Steve was insistent that I get up and do this right on the spot, so I would. And you know, it was amazing. I'd go to wherever this particular person was amongst his peers; I'd go in and interrupt a meeting and say, "I understand you've done this electronic change order, and it's taken two weeks out of the schedule. Great job – it's really going to help us get the product out earlier and make more money for the company earlier. Absolutely tremendous job."

I would never just say "great job". I would show people that I understood the impact of what they were doing, and I'd reinforce how it was going to help us. Word about these public recognition talks spread like wildfire through the organization. People want this kind of recognition. They want to help. They want to be recognized for doing a good job. Everybody wants to be recognized for making a positive difference. This became one of the major drivers for change in the organization: people wanted to be recognized by senior management within the company for the fact that they were making a difference on Quality and Time-To-Market.

Once I realized how important this simple kind of recognition was, I also started doing elevator speeches – literally. I'd get in the elevator going up to my office or to a meeting, and there would be R&D people in the elevator. I may not have known their names but I'd ask them who they were, where they worked, what they were working on. Whatever it happened to be, I'd take the time of that elevator ride to tell them how important their work was, and why it was important for them to focus on this, and to figure out how they could get their product out within the least amount of time. Some people were a bit surprised that the VP was telling them this. Again, it was this kind of recognition, and reinforcing how everyone was important, that was really key. A lot of people walked out of the elevator really jazzed and proud about the importance of what they were doing. I believe this is where motivation comes from.

I'd go into a lunchroom or cafeteria and purposely sit with some engineers who still thought Quality and Time-To-Market was an "OR function" not an "AND function", and listen to what they had to say. Then I'd communicate my belief that there were things that they could do to shorten the timeframe. I would also acknowledge that there are some things that we couldn't do, like release the product before all the bugs are were out. Some of them got it and some of them didn't and some probably don't to this day, but that was my job – full-time motivator and spokesperson for my mantra.

Steve's Thoughts On This:

Geoff was a really quick study when it came to the power of using positive feedback. Like many executives, Geoff is a pretty humble guy and at first didn't really understand how important it was to people for the Vice President to make a point of congratulating them for something. There were very few times that I had to go and drag him out of his office to go and recognize a person or team for something. Once I had done that a couple of times he saw the big impact that he was having on them and he started doing it on his own. He really surprised me with his "elevator chats", using his elevator time to talk to people. I thought it was a brilliant idea.

Key Learnings

Company

- Positive feedback is fast, free, and endless. When done well it has a higher impact on achieving business results than tangible rewards.

Change Champion

- With title in the organization comes power, whether you want it or not. Remember that you cast a long shadow and that people watch you very closely – the words you choose, your body language, who you sit with at lunch.

- If you are going to lead change, be sure to give lots of positive reinforcement along the way. Do it as soon as you hear about someone taking positive action. Don't wait for the end result; recognize people at every step along the way.

- Feedback must be specific to be effective.

Change Agent

- The power of positive feedback is in the timing. The closer the positive feedback (reinforcement) is to the behavior, the more impactful it will be. Traditional reward systems like bonuses or pay raises are often too far removed from the actual behavior to shape behavior effectively.

Chapter 13

After The Cows Went Home – Geoff

WITH THE SACRED Cow workshops behind us and everyone in R&D experiencing the effects, it was time to reap the benefits. We continued to hold Town Hall meetings, where I emphasized where we were going and how we were doing. I continued to share my Quality and Time-To-Market mantra every time I talked to people in the R&D organization – even though I got sick of saying the same things over and over and was surprised at how often I had to say them before everybody finally got it! We also used email newsletters and bulletin boards to celebrate people who had killed Cows, improved Time-To-Market, and made progress towards improving Quality.

People were questioning why we always did things the way we'd always done them in the past. Steve had come up with this theme of "Sacred Cows" for the CPL workshop, and we used this cow theme at the Town Halls and in the newsletters. We talked about people who were doing new things and killing off Sacred Cows in order to improve Quality and Time-To-Market. If you killed off a Sacred Cow, you got a mug with a cow on it. We had cow mailboxes, cardboard cows stuck in the lawn out front, and pictures of cows in the hallway – these things were everywhere. We stocked up on cow paraphernalia and kept reinforcing people by giving the stuff out. Some people thought it was a little corny, but the Sacred Cow theme was one that everyone could relate to. It kept our momentum going, and lots of people had fun with it. We encouraged people to question things, to make a difference, and communicate it when they did. These things reinforced our change strategy. Once you build momentum for change, you have to keep putting effort into it or it will die.

People started coming up with new processes to eliminate bugs. One particularly effective thing they did was to develop a single test plan so there wasn't any overlap between groups. Testers and designers no longer "threw the product over the wall" from R&D to Product Verification. R&D would test a portion of the product, Product Verification would test another portion, and then together they would test the whole thing. It seems really simple in retrospect, but people have to be reinforced for these kinds of behaviors and motivated to do them. The Sacred Cow workshops had got people thinking this way.

As another example, people started questioning why we did field trials with certain products. We had some mature products that still went through a controlled six-week field trial even though we never found faults with them. But it was the way we had always done it. So our people tackled this issue in a smart way on a case-by-case basis and they took about six weeks out of the delivery schedule.

The CDI was enhanced over time, to include an algorithm that could detect a project's likelihood of having a bug discovered once it was in the field. So, even though something tested clean, if it failed the CDI algorithm, the engineers would look deeper for a lurking problem in the system.

Hearing these things, I would congratulate the teams and communicate these kinds of success stories back to the rest of the engineers about ways we were reducing Time-To-Market without affecting Quality.

Steve's Thoughts On This:

A year after the debut of the Tucson Tape, Mitel's dealers met again – this time in Puerto Rico at the Westin Rio Mar. We made another videotape with the dealers, asking the same 10 questions as before. The results were astounding. It was a love-fest as the dealers heaped praise on what we had done. The Quality problems in the field had dried up. New features were coming out faster. Their issues were being addressed at breakneck speed. When asked what else we could do for them, many dealers were speechless. They were spending less time and money fixing problems. They were selling more products and, of course, they were making a lot more money. The airing of the "Rio Tape" back in Kanata was a happy event, and great reinforcement for those who had done so much hard work. It was a win-win for all.

Beyond Rio

The "Tucson Tape" and the follow up "Rio Tape" confirmed our intuition that strengthening the link between the voice-of-customer and R&D would result in better products and increased customer satisfaction. Rather than make a third videotape, we upped the ante and began an annual Customer Forum for our engineers to meet directly with field technicians who worked for our customers. Every year we would offer an all-expenses-paid trip to Kanata for one senior technician from each of our six biggest Dealers. These techs would spend two days in a conference room with 15 or 20 of our engineers where they would discuss problems in the field and ways to resolve them. I remember sitting in the first session as one technician described a problem and what he wanted done about it. Our engineers scratched their heads and said, "Man, that will require months of redesign." The technician went on to explain more fully what the customer wanted, to which the engineers replied, "Well, if that's all they want you can have it next week." With this one conversation the entire Customer Forum had just paid for itself. That single conversation became somewhat legendary in R&D as it taught our engineers the importance of finding out what the customer really wanted. Often, that made it easy for them to deliver simple, quick solutions that made everyone look good.

- Steve

The R&D department was no longer viewed as the company laggard. Gone was the Mitel shuffle – R&D employees walked briskly with heads held high. We had a Friday Social with beer and snacks that made other departments jealous. We were the "can-do" people, the innovators and smart risk-takers who were motivated and having a lot of fun at the same time.

As a company, our profitability ramped back up as well. At the Sacred Cow workshops during the pink slip exercise, Kirk had told everyone about the one half percent profitability of the Systems division. Two years after we started the organizational change work, the company profitability hit a healthy 20%.

The Sacred Cows had been put out to pasture.

CHAPTER 14

Outcomes

COMPANY - MITEL

What Worked

In the two years during R&D's transformation, Mitel's Systems division increased its bottom-line profit from $2 million to $80 million without making any significant acquisitions or other structural changes. Better quality products delivered on time helped to drive and increase sales. This, coupled with improved efficiencies in the development and testing processes in R&D, meant lower support costs. Mitel was now selling competitive products, including VoIP, that were delivered on time and ready to meet market demand for increased features and functionality. Once again, the company earned a solid reputation in the marketplace. Mitel was able to catch the wave of increased sales in the telecommunication industry at that time, with products that were proven to be Y2K-compatible and with far fewer bugs escaping the lab.

What Didn't Work

All departments were not aligned and ready for the new VoIP products.

CHANGE CHAMPION - GEOFF

What Worked

We got the Quality issue fixed. The voice of the customer was clearly understood by R&D. The CDI target was adopted; the engineers stuck to it, and even advanced the CDI itself by building in a prediction algorithm. The dealers were astounded at the improvements we made in Quality over the two years.

We improved the Time-To-Market for new product releases by a factor of two. The sense of urgency initially instilled by the R&D clock became entrenched within the department.

R&D went from being the black sheep of the company to the "can-do" group in a couple of short years.

Convergence of voice and data took longer than anyone had predicted, which allowed us time to define which strategy to pursue and to figure out a new architecture. In the end, we met the new competition head on with a market-leading, fully featured VoIP system.

What Didn't Work

Outside of R&D, there was definite misalignment between when the IP product was ready and when the rest of the company was ready, specifically Marketing and Sales. The red flag that I noticed at Demo Day should have been a flag for me to turn my focus from my R&D organization to work on my peers. I should have been poking my nose into other departments sooner in order to pressure them to reskill their organization in a similar way to what we had done in R&D.

Geoff's Final Advice To Change Champions:

- Defining a strategy is the easy part. In order to execute your strategy you're probably going to need to change behaviors. Getting the right behaviors to support the strategy is the hardest and most important part of execution.

- Your job is to be a full-time evangelist and motivator for change.

- Organizational Development is the way to fix cultural problems systemically and make them last.

- Don't wait for the big home run; implement your changes in baby steps.

- Challenge and empower your people. Remember what Margaret Mead once said: "Never doubt that a small group of thoughtful, committed citizens can change the world; indeed, it's the only thing that ever has."

- Recognize and reinforce your people for moving the yardsticks forward.

- Change only keeps its momentum as long as you continue to reinforce it. It takes much longer than you think for new behaviors to become ingrained and to stick.

- Be prepared to be tested personally. Accept the organization's challenges and be prepared to participate yourself by walking the talk.

Change Agent - Steve

What Worked

In the end, I was really proud of the business outcome and the change in profitability. The high support costs and slow release of products were going to kill the Systems division, and the work that Geoff and I did resulted in the lion's share of the improved results.

I am also proud of the Tucson Tape, the R&D clock, the Sacred Cow workshops, Demo Day, and the work that my team did to support the CDI. I am proud of the amount of work that we were able to do on a shoestring budget. Last but certainly not least, I am proud of the partnership that Geoff and I formed to do all of this with help from my friend and mentor Dr. Mike Miles.

What Didn't Work

It would have been nice to build some earlier positive bridges with the HR team. During my six years at Mitel, I went back to night school and got an HR certification because as the work continued I needed to understand their world better.

I would have also liked the opportunity to extend the change work beyond R&D into other departments. There were a few areas where I managed to do so but they were small compared to the work that I did in R&D.

Without a doubt, my biggest regret is not hiring OD support earlier. I think that despite all of our success, we left opportunities on the table because there wasn't enough of me to go around to support all of the changes. Thanks to Beverley Patwell and Chris O'Gorman for all that you did. I just wish that I had hired you sooner.

STEVE'S FINAL ADVICE TO CHANGE AGENTS:

- Be sure that you have a willing and able Change Champion to partner with.

- Do lots of diagnostics to be sure that you understand the culture, history and collective motives of the organization before moving to action.

- Keep it simple in all interventions and communications.

- Develop a short list of issues to tackle.

- Focus on the few critical-to-success behaviors that need to change.

- It takes a long time to get from awareness to action. Be patient and come at it from different angles.

- Use lots of positive feedback and recognition to shape behavior and celebrate wins.

- Use visible scoreboards and give ownership to those who affect the numbers.

Epilogue

SO WHAT HAPPENED to the little company that could? Much has changed since the Cows went home. The VoIP systems were developed and launched as planned and form the bulk of Mitel sales today. Riding a wave of profitability, in the year 2000 Mitel was split in half. The semiconductor business remains a publicly traded company called Zarlink Semiconductor. The Systems division of Mitel was sold to Terry Matthews — one of the original founders of the company. Terry turned the Systems division into a private company and renamed it Mitel Networks.

In 2008, Mitel Networks bought one of its largest competitors, Inter-Tel. Terry Matthews is still a major shareholder of the combined firm and Mitel Networks continues to execute its strategy of building and selling Voice Over IP phone systems and business applications.

PART 2

THE METHOD:
TOOLS AND TECHNIQUES

CHAPTER 15

Principles, Models And Tools – Steve

WHILE PART 1 of this book tells the story of *what* happened at Mitel, Part 2 presents *how* and *why* we chose the approach to change that we did.

In the next few chapters we will explain our guiding principles, the change models we use, and then we will revisit parts of the Mitel story to show how these things apply "in real life". We will describe each model separately and how we used it, but you will quickly see that, like a jigsaw puzzle, these models overlap and interconnect in a way that creates synergy and momentum for change in a powerful and positive way.

In our organizational change work, Geoff and I employ methods that are anchored in years of behavior-based scientific research and practices. Our approach uses quantifiable measures and achieves tangible business results. We are guided by three specific principles, which embody our overall philosophy:

1. *Successful organizational change programs are aligned to support business goals.*

Change for its own sake is misguided and irresponsible.

Successful organizational change leads to a measurable increase in a significant business result in a way that employees want to, rather than have to, participate.

2. *Successful organizational change is focused on changing <u>behaviors</u>, not changing <u>people</u>.*

This is an important distinction. Organizational Development is not about manipulating people or changing their beliefs. It is about creating an environment whereby people can – and want to – work together to achieve business goals. We do this by influencing what people say and what people do.

3. *Focusing on behavior is the key element in making effective change.*

Behavior is simply what a person says or does – period. Understanding what behavior is, and how to describe behavior effectively to others, is key not only to making change, but also to all aspects of leadership. Chapter 16 explains this fundamental concept in detail.

We apply these guiding principles within a framework for organizational change, which consists of four elements. In Chapter 17 we will expand on each of these four elements, explaining what each one is and how to deploy it.

1. *Leadership Readiness:* having a champion for change at the top of the organization.

2. *Organizational Diagnostics:* tools to measure the culture and the change process.

3. *Change Events:* activities specifically designed to make change happen *with* people rather than *at* them.

4. *Sustainability:* actions and measures that make the gains of change last.

At the very end of the book, we provide a Change Assessment Worksheet, to help organizations determine their own readiness for change based on the four elements of the change framework.

Our toolkit for organizational change draws on four theoretical models, which we apply in practical ways:

1. The ABC model of behavior

2. The *DCOM*® model[7]

3. Kurt Lewin's "Unfreeze – Move – Refreeze" model[8]

4. Richard Beckhard and David Gliecher's formula for change[9]

These models are effective, and have been proven to work in real business situations. They worked at Mitel and they have worked in many other organizations around the world. In Chapters 16, 17 and 18 we will explain the theory behind each model and show how it was applied at Mitel.

Chapter 16

Understanding Behavior – Steve

ORGANIZATIONAL CHANGE, ORGANIZATIONAL excellence, leadership, personal and professional performance are all functions of behavior. Improving any of these things means either shaping or entirely changing key behaviors – those that are critical to the success of achieving specific goals. Understanding behavior is central to making change happen and to sustaining change, yet the meaning of the word "behavior" is often misconstrued. So what is behavior in its simplest form?

DEFINITION:
Behavior is anything that a person says or does – period.

Using the "say-and-do" definition means that behavior can be observed, measured, and counted. Fact-based observations of behavior are not open to interpretation.

This is important because the Change Champion and the Change Agent must agree on the specific behaviors that need to be shaped or changed to achieve specific business outcomes. Furthermore, individuals need to know exactly what is expected of them – even more so in times of change.

Dangers

Some of the typical obstacles or "dangers" that get in the way of fact-based behavior discussions are:

- Use of labels and extrapolation
- Use of body language
- Use of exaggeration

Dangers of Using Labels and Extrapolation

One of the greatest dangers that we see in our work is the use of labels in the attempt to describe behavior. When asked to articulate the "critical-to-success" behaviors they need from their employees, business leaders will often say things like: "Jim needs more leadership presence", "I want Sally to motivate her people", or "the Sales team needs to pick up their game". All three of these examples are label-based, and do not describe any behaviors that a change agent can use. Consider these two statements:

"Bill sat quietly through the meeting with his arms crossed."

"Bill really checked out during the meeting – his body language was closed and he was clearly not in favor of the ideas presented."

"Bill sat quietly through the meeting with his arms crossed" is an objective, and fact-based description of behavior. This is a clear observation of what Bill did. It meets the "say-and-do" criteria.

"Bill really checked out during the meeting – his body language was closed and he was clearly not in favor of the ideas presented" is neither objective nor does it meet the "say-and-do" criteria of behavior. This description uses subjective labels ("body language was closed") and goes on to further extrapolate meaning from the label ("he was clearly not in favor of the ideas presented"). Extrapolation is a form of interpretation whereby we assign meaning to things that we observe. Attempting to extrapolate meaning from Bill's behavior is both dangerous – potentially leading to conflict or miscommunication – and unfair. Bill might have been cold, or perhaps he was just resting his arms in a way that was comfortable to him as he listened quietly. As a quick check, extrapolation has occurred any time that you can insert the word "therefore" into a sentence. So, in the example above: "his body language was closed *therefore* he was clearly not in favor of…"

Behavior is not accurately or objectively described by words like "attitude", "on the ball", "negative personality", "keener", "lazy", "ambitious" or "dysfunctional". These words and phrases are labels, which are open to a wide amount of interpretation and do not serve us well when we are conducting organizational diagnostics or providing feedback.

Dangers of Using Body Language

There have been a great many books written on body language, and most lack any basis on scientific evidence. Labeling behavior based on body language is just as dangerous and unfair as the labeling and extrapolation discussed above. You cannot tell what someone is thinking based on their body language. However, observation of body language behaviors may provide clues that can serve as good conversation starters.

For example: "Bill, I see that you have been sitting quietly with your arms folded throughout the meeting. We would like to get everyone's opinion on this new idea. Tell us what you think about what has been presented here today." This is an effective way to use Bill's observable body language behavior as a conversation starter to clarify Bill's thinking.

Dangers of Using Exaggeration

Another common pitfall to accurately describing behavior is exaggeration. The statement "I've told you a million times not to interrupt me during a meeting" is neither objective nor acceptable as a description of behavior.

"You interrupted me three times during the meeting" is factual and not open to interpretation. Using dates, counts, times and other measures are powerful elements of behavior observation and helpful to shape behavior.

NORMS[10] And "Say-and-do" Tests

Using labels, exaggeration, interpretation and extrapolation to give someone feedback will often sound like a personal attack. Instead of using these, it is important for everyone involved in a change initiative to learn how to pinpoint behaviors. There are two simple methods of testing whether or not a behavior is pinpointed:

- NORMS, and
- The "say-and-do" test.

NORMS stands for:

N = Not an interpretation. The behavior description must be factual and not a label.

O = Observable. If it is a behavior, you can observe something said or done.

R = Reliable. Two people would come to the same conclusion when independently observing and describing the behavior.

M = Measurable. The number of occurrences of the behavior can be counted.

S = Specific. A specific and pinpointed behavior is observed.

Applying NORMS is a way to verify that a behavior is being discussed.

Another approach is to use the mental "say-and-do" test. Is what you are about to say something that the person has said or done? Is it something you want the other person to say or do? If so, you are talking in behavior terms and not using labels, exaggeration or extrapolation.

Objective and pinpointed behavior-based statements look like this:

- "I noticed that you began processing the next stack of invoices without being asked."

- "During your presentation tomorrow I would like you look at your audience and over the 30 minutes, make eye contact with every person in the room."

- "You completed the compressor repair and tested it before taking your break."

- "This is the third time this week that you have returned more than 10 minutes late from lunch."

- "I want you to say four positive things to your team mates today."

How This Worked at Mitel

A good example of pinpointing specific behaviors is evident in the Customer Dissatisfaction Index (CDI) story. Once Geoff set the CDI target at 10,000, the R&D managers worked with their teams to pinpoint several key behaviors that were critical to achieving the goal. There was a big "ah-ha" moment when Technical Support questioned the "first-in/first-served" rule to fixing problems. They thought this was a behavior that was required of them. When it was made clear to everyone that the "first-in, first-served" rule was actually a Sacred Cow and not a rule at all, their behavior shifted immediately and they started tackling the highest-impact bugs based on their CDI score rather than what was sequentially next on the bug list. Selecting a bug to work on based on the CDI score was a specific behavior.

To achieve the CDI of less than 10,000, the Technical Support managers adopted a critical-to-success behavior of holding weekly CDI meetings, which in turn spawned several key supporting behaviors. Every week, each group who affected the CDI calculated their number (a behavior), calculated what they thought the number was going to be the following week (a behavior), and then attended a meeting to disclose their numbers and action plans (two more behaviors). The total CDI number was calculated each week and plotted on a graph. All of these were critical and specific behaviors, supported by the managers, which helped to achieve the business goal of improved product Quality.

The ABC Model of Behavior

The ABC model is frequently used by behavioral scientists to describe things that *prompt* behavior (Antecedents) and the things that happen as a *result* of behavior (Consequences). It is known as the Antecedent – Behavior – Consequence model.

According to the ABC model, every behavior is prompted by some kind of trigger called an antecedent. Antecedents take many forms, including:

- An email request for action,
- A note on the fridge saying "take out the trash today,"
- The reading on a speedometer.

Similarly, following every behavior is a consequence. Consequences are either positive or negative. Consequences can come from other people, or from within ourselves, or from the surrounding environment. Consequences take many forms, including:

- Words of praise or criticism,
- Gifts,
- Burning yourself on a hot stove.

Seeing a traffic light turn amber as you approach an intersection (A) prompts the driver to place their foot on the brake pedal (B) so that the car stops safely before the intersection thereby avoiding a collision (C). Antecedent – Behavior – Consequence.

The most powerful consequences are often the ones that we give to ourselves. Embarrassment, pride, joy and humiliation are very strong and powerful influencers of behavior. Someone who has suffered humiliation as a consequence of his or her behavior is unlikely to repeat the same behavior again. Conversely, if we can create a scenario where a person's behavior will result in feelings of joy or pride, they will be very likely to repeat the same behavior that brought them these consequences.

In our personal and professional lives we can influence the behavior of others through the use of antecedents and consequences. It is believed that consequences are about four times as powerful as antecedents when influencing behavior. This is called the 80/20 rule of behavior: 20% of reoccurring behaviors are a result of antecedents and 80% of reoccurring behaviors are a result of consequences. This is not to say that antecedents can be neglected entirely, however. Telling someone what you want them to do is an antecedent and a necessary condition to getting the behavior at all.

How This Worked at Mitel

As we focused on the key business outcomes of improved Quality and Time-To-Market we used a number of antecedents and consequences. Some of the antecedents were the showings of the Tucson Tape, putting up the R&D clock and the bulletin board, organizing Demo Day, and holding the CPL Workshops. All of these antecedents were selected to prompt or activate new behaviors. While they were designed as antecedents, all of these interventions offered consequences as well.

Consequences Resulting From the Tucson Tape

On the Tucson Tape, dealers spoke of employees by name and in so doing, they delivered consequences for past behaviors. Some were positive (people felt good about the things that were said about them) and some were negative (people felt embarrassed about the comments). Pride was either reinforced or threatened, but in either case, the problems of the customer became much higher in the consciousness of R&D. Most of the engineers — with the exception of those who thought the customers were wrong — changed their behaviors to work harder and smarter to fix product problems. From this motivation came the development of the CDI. With the adoption of the CDI to fix field problems, even more behaviors changed. The resulting business objective was better product Quality.

Consequences Resulting From The R&D Clock and Project Bulletin Board

The obvious negative consequence came from the big red X that went beside the first project that missed its delivery date. However, this did shift behaviors and subsequent projects achieved their targeted dates.

Consequences Resulting From Demo Day

There were two really positive consequences that came out of Demo Day. First, our engineers got a lot of praise from others as they demonstrated their work. Along with this praise from their audiences, the day fostered a lot of personal pride in this group. We gave them the opportunity to brag about their well-earned accomplishments. The second big positive consequence came from the learning and discoveries that took place during the day. Many engineers were really happy to have found bits of hardware or software that already existed with other teams that were going to make their job easier.

Consequences resulting from the CPL Workshops

The Sacred Cow or CPL workshops offered many positive consequence to all: employees got direct exposure to Geoff and Kirk who personally led sessions and employees were able to spend time putting together action plans for their return to the office.

SUMMARY: UNDERSTANDING BEHAVIOR

- Behavior is what someone says or does – period.

- Using NORMS or the "say-and-do" test to either provide instructions or feedback will remove ambiguity, clarify expectations for success and, in so doing, lessen resistance. Labeling, making assumptions, exaggeration, and false interpretation of observable behaviors such as body language are all major impediments to changing behavior. These common pitfalls decrease the level of buy-in because they sound like personal attacks. Providing expectations or feedback in a pinpointed manner increases the level of buy-in.

- Behavior is triggered or activated by antecedents, and every behavior results in a consequence to the performer. This consequence can be internally generated or come from the external environment.

- When trying to achieve a business objective, begin with the outcome in mind and then work backward to find the behaviors that are critical to achieve this goal.

CHAPTER 17

Framework For Organizational Change – Steve

A SUCCESSFUL ORGANIZATIONAL change program does not set about to change people. It seeks to influence their behavior to improve an important business result. There are four critical elements to any organizational change program. We call this the Framework for Organizational Change:

1. *Leadership Readiness:* Having a champion for change at the top of the organization.

2. *Organizational Diagnostics:* Tools to measure the culture and the change process.

3. *Behavior Change Events:* Activities specifically designed to make change happen *with* people rather than *at* them.

4. *Sustainability:* Activities and measures undertaken to make the gains of change last.

1. Leadership Readiness: Having a Champion for Change at the Top of the Organization

People often ask whether change needs to be "led from the top or from the bottom of an organization". A better question to ask is whether or not there is *support* for change at the top of the organization. Without the support and commitment of a Change Champion at the organization's senior level, large-scale organizational change is doomed to failure. Change often involves reassigning people, retooling reporting relationships, creating new cross-functional processes, communicating direction, and changing consequence systems. People at the top of the organization own these types of things. Change can also have many political implications. A wise Change Champion will be on the lookout for these kinds of issues and work with his / her peers to navigate the political waters around them. Senior executives are people too and can feel jealous, threatened or sidelined by changes in the organization.

The matter of leading change is a broader issue. Change needs to be led at all levels in the organization by employees who are engaged and motivated to make changes in everyday behaviors.

Change is sometimes initiated through the Human Resources department, which raises a caution flag. HR often has information to signal that organizational change is necessary, but as a support function HR may not be the best group to lead change. The same is true of other support functions like Finance and Information Technology (IT). Change driven by a support function runs the risk of allowing line leaders to abdicate their responsibility and commitment to the change effort. In our experience, HR or other support functions can be great brokers of change and suppliers of change expertise and tools, but

Change Champions will have the most success if they come from line organizations and operational groups.

How This Worked at Mitel

Geoff was clearly the Change Champion of the R&D organization and he had two well-articulated business goals in mind: fix product Quality and improve Time-To-Market. As a Vice President, he had the title and authority to make change. He had the ability to see the company with fresh eyes, and was also politically savvy.

Throughout the Mitel turnaround, Geoff got the support and involvement of CEO Kirk Mandy and other organizational leaders as well. He provided air cover from other groups who resisted the change effort and he fought for budget dollars when needed. Geoff walked the talk by making tough decisions like the one at The Barons meeting when he let go the Head of Software Design. He walked the talk by personally killing off Sacred Cows like the travel requisition process. Over and over again he talked about Quality and Time-To-Market. Over and over again he would help people rebalance priorities so that R&D continued to deliver existing products while developing new products. His ongoing positive reinforcement had an enormously motivating effect on people.

2. Organizational Diagnostics: Tools to measure the culture and the change process

Conducting good organizational diagnostics is vital to any change program. Just as a doctor would never treat a patient without first performing a patient assessment, an Organizational Development professional should never initiate a change program without thoroughly assessing the organization's culture. While a patient's ongoing care may change, depending on how he/she is reacting to treatment, the same is true for organizations: the change program will require constant monitoring for adjustment. Just as the long-term health of a patient may depend on establishing new lifestyle habits, so an organization will need to entrench new habits and behaviors in order to sustain the change.

Ideally, organizational diagnostics should be conducted during three key points in a change program:

- Pre-change: to understand the status quo culture and business goals.

- During change: to determine whether the change events are having the desired effect.

- Post change: to measure how far the organization has moved, and to determine what is necessary to sustain the change.

In analyzing organizational diagnostics, it is the role of the OD professional to:

- Differentiate between symptoms and root causes, and

- Determine if the data are relevant to achieving an important business goal.

How This Worked at Mitel

Before designing or carrying out any activities to initiate change, I did a lot of diagnostic work to understand the R&D culture. This partial list of diagnostic data shows the wide range of data-gathering tools used, and the types of symptoms that showed up in R&D:

Diagnostic Used	What Was Revealed
Observation of the facilities, the "Mitel shuffle," walkabouts and interactions with employees from different departments.	Indicated the degree of decay and disempowerment within the company. These also showed how deeply ingrained the negative parts of the culture were.
Dr. Mike's Culture Study: the "Around Here We Behave As If" survey.	Indicated decision-making processes were missing or broken; inappropriate behaviors were tolerated; people felt frustrated.
The hallway poster campaign ("Dumb things we do around here").	The time it took for employees to respond indicated that this was an introspective, deep-thinking organization that wasn't going to react to things quickly. Use of yellow stickies indicated pride: people didn't want to get "caught" writing on the poster. The types of responses indicated feelings of disempowerment.
Geoff's red-hair rants.	Revealed key business issues to work on.
The customer letter to the CEO provided by Geoff and the newspaper article about Mitel in the business section.	Showed the degree of the loss of Mitel's reputation in the marketplace and the transparency of the organization's problems to the outside business world.
Meeting with the director of HR (the FIFO conversation).	Showed the Sacred Cows that existed in HR and how unlikely HR was to provide support for the change work.
Observations of behaviors in meetings.	Indicated there were unhealthy behaviors at all levels that would require coaching.
Elite Dealers' Council meeting and the Tucson Tape.	Showed the magnitude of the business crisis.

From this data about the symptoms and issues within the culture of R&D, we were able to determine the root causes:

- The near-death experience had created a culture that stunted creativity and where people carefully followed even outmoded processes and stopped asking, "Why?"

- The voice of the customer was not getting through to the engineers in R&D; they had no sense of urgency or clarity about the business and what it was going to take to increase customer satisfaction (customer here meaning both the dealers who sold the products and the end customers who purchased and used the products).

- People were not held accountable for Quality or delivery schedules.

Mitel was suffering from what we call "the boiled frog syndrome". The anecdotal frog story goes like this: if you drop a frog into a hot pan of water, the frog will jump out. However if you put a frog in a cool pan of water and slowly heat it up, the frog will keep trying to adapt to the changing environment until it is too late and it dies. The moral of the story is quite simple: when we walk into a new situation, we can be sharply affected by the environment or culture; however, those who have been living in the environment for a long time are less likely to be sensitive to these issues. Mitel had become a company of boiled frogs. The culture was apathetic, lethargic and stagnant, but the employees could not see it, or if they did, they were too ingrained in old habits to change. Thanks to his ability to still see the company with fresh eyes, Geoff saw the need for change. As a new hire to the company I had been dropped into the "pan of hot water" and saw clearly the unhealthy cultural underpinnings of R&D. As leaders of the change program, it was our job to signal the danger to those who had been swimming there for a long time.

After identifying the root causes of this situation, and reviewing the business goals of Quality and Time-To-Market, I came to several conclusions about the required change program:

- Pride was the most powerful consequence to help shape behavior in R&D. This was the lever that was used to fix Time-To-Market and Quality via the project clock and CDI respectively.

- R&D needed a powerful event to break the Organizational Immune System™ and give people a sense of urgency about the business issues. We needed to get employees open to change and to shake off the near-death experience. This is why the CPL workshop included the "pink slip" exercise as a shock factor and the detailed simulation as an all important deflection exercise.

- To help this group regain its confidence, every win had to be celebrated. This is why Demo Day was developed, and why I dragged Geoff out of his office every time I heard something positive had happened, and why there was cake on the day the CDI broke the 10,000 threshold.

As the change program progressed, we relied on continuous observation and discussion to help monitor whether or not we were effecting the required change. In particular, we watched the project management delivery schedule and the CDI weekly score.

We successfully tapped into the expertise of our HR representative who helped us to monitor the R&D employee attrition rate to see if any high performers were leaving. Over time, we developed and deployed an employee satisfaction survey as well. Although it did not provide us with a continuous stream of data, it did give us an annual snapshot of how people were coping with the change. I even kept a tally of how many times I saw anyone run anywhere on the Mitel campus – run to a meeting, run to catch an elevator, run to see if someone was still at their desk to share good news with them. Although not terribly scientific, it did give me a gut feel for the level of visible engagement behaviors that were taking root.

3. Behavior Change Events: Making Change Happen With People Rather Than At Them

Almost every book on change will explain how important it is to involve everyone when making large-scale changes. Where many organizations fail is in making the distinction between "involvement" and "awareness"; with ample communication it is relatively easy to make people aware that change is coming. However, awareness does not always result in buy-in. Involvement results in buy-in, but it is far more time-consuming to get everyone involved.

In order to get people involved, and therefore committed to making change, it is vital to remember: "change is a door that is opened from the inside".[11] People don't resist change; they resist *being* changed. A successful change initiative creates the right environment to enroll people in making changes happen. Countless change efforts have failed as a result of those with more power trying to force change on others.

Along with the ABC Model of Behavior described in Chapter 16, three behavioral models provide the tools to conduct a change program in which people are enrolled and involved. The models are:

- DCOM®,
- Kirk Lewin's Unfreeze – Move – Refreeze, and
- Richard Beckhard and David Gleicher's Formula for Change.

DCOM®

In her book, *Unlock Behavior, Unleash Profits*, Dr. Leslie Braksick uses the acronym DCOM® as a methodology to set people up to succeed. DCOM® stands for:

- **Direction**: giving clear directions for the completion of a task or expectations of others.
- **Competence**: ensuring that a person tasked with something has been trained with the skills to successfully carry it out.
- **Opportunity**: ensuring that the time, tools and other resources required to complete a task are available to the performer.
- **Motivation**: ensuring that there are net positive consequences to the performer for completing a task.

The DCOM® diagnostic is a simple and effective way to check if the antecedents and consequences are in place for people to be successful. Without the antecedents of clear direction, skills, and resources, a person can't do what is asked of them. Motivation reinforces appropriate behavior with positive consequences and discourages inappropriate behavior with negative consequences.

When a person has the <u>D</u>irection, <u>C</u>ompetence and <u>O</u>pportunity, but still refuses to engage in a required behavior, this is called a "won't-do" scenario and is a function of the balance of consequences associated with the task. As they assess whether or not to engage in a behavior, the performer will evaluate whether the new behavior will result in an increase in the level of positive consequences to them or a decrease in the level of negative consequences to them. Those who are reluctant to change their behaviors are the kinds of people that Geoff referred to as "the stragglers". They knew what was expected of them, they had the skills and all the resources, but they were not willing to change the way they did things.

How This Worked at Mitel

We invested a lot of time in the <u>D</u>irection, making Geoff's expectations for improved Quality and Time-To-Market clear. The frequent Town Halls helped to achieve this but the biggest thing to help us with <u>D</u>, <u>C</u> and <u>O</u> was the CPL workshops.

The CPL workshops provided a highly concentrated environment where all aspects of the **DCOM**® model were worked. Starting the workshops with the simulation really helped to crack the Organizational Immune System™ so that people were open to hearing and accepting what was expected of them. Direction was further clarified through presentations done by Geoff and Kirk. The change management skills taught at the workshop addressed the Competence gap for changing behavior, and the Sacred Cows that senior leaders killed ensured that the employees had the Opportunity, or resources, to make the change. People were Motivated by senior leaders killing off Sacred Cows on the spot. The inclusiveness of taking everyone off-site for three days was also incredibly motivating. People got to do something very different for a few days, they got direct access to senior company leaders, and the "real work" that got done in preparing action plans was a vote of confidence in the organization.

The project management list that had indicated that every one of R&D's projects was running late was also a prime opportunity to do a *DCOM*® analysis. We quickly determined that the Direction, Competence and Opportunity were all pretty much in place. What was missing was a set of motivating consequences. No one was being held accountable for project dates being missed, no bonuses were affected, and no one was disciplined. There were no negative consequences for missing a date, nor were there any significant celebrations (positive consequences) for achieving a product launch on time. Instead there were some inappropriate positive consequences for missing dates, like the ability to work at a slower pace. Submitting pieces of a project late was an acceptable and self-rewarding behavior.

The R&D clock became a Motivator because it delivered the negative consequence of putting pride in jeopardy. It made missed dates visible and the people associated with them visible too. With the clock, people also lost the freedom to work at their own speed. Although it provided a negative motivation – something to be avoided – the clock was effective.

Kurt Lewin's Unfreeze – Change – Refreeze Model

Lewin believed that to change an organization, it first had to get "unstuck" or "unfrozen" from the bonds of current routine. Some kind of strong external stimulus or rapid change in the environment is needed to break through. Once the pattern of status quo routine is changed, the organization can be redirected and new, more effective, behaviors can take root as the culture settles in or refreezes.

How This Worked at Mitel

Before the change program, the culture at Mitel was strongly entrenched and so unhealthy it was unable to meet the critical challenges facing the company. The Organizational Immune System™ was so resilient it required a significant push to begin the unfreezing process.

The Tucson Tape provided the first big push. The voice of the customers spoke loudly and directly to the engineers, which inspired most of them to rush back to work on fixing product problems.

The CPL workshops continued the unfreezing process, in particular through the simulation and the slideshow of R&D's worn and cluttered work environment. The slideshow highlighted the level of decay in the environment, and prompted the realization that maybe other things – like processes – were also decayed.

The simulation used at the CPL workshops was centered on accurate problem-solving, dissemination of complex communication, managing risk, and quick decision-making – exactly what R&D needed. We would close out the debrief of each simulation in the same way, with one simple question: "How is our work in R&D like what you experienced today?" In each of the five workshops there was a magical "ah-ha!" moment.

People began effusively telling us how much this was like the things they were facing on a daily basis, and how important it was for the company to change.

Following the CPL workshops, the organization was able to move, as evidenced by the killing of Sacred Cows, creative problem-solving like the CDI, and new approaches to processes like field trials.

Designing An Effective Change Event – Using A Deflection Exercise

You might think that if you sit down with a group of smart people and explain logically which unhealthy aspects of their organization's culture need changing, you would be able to engage them in a discussion about how to go about changing these aspects. Experience says otherwise. People are frozen into patterns of behavior by the current culture, which is reinforced by the Organizational Immune System™. When a new consultant or new employee tries to explain to employees what is inappropriate about the current culture, they will be met with a lot of defensive reactions. Employees are doing the best they can in their environment and can't see the problems as clearly as an outsider. This is where a "deflection exercise" such as a simulation can be very effective.

A successful simulation will expose people to an unrelated environment that requires the same type of changes as the ailing organization. There are two things to look for when choosing an effective simulation. First, the basis of the simulation must be entirely unrelated to the day-to-day activities of the employees. For example, if working with a group of hospital workers, a care-giving/medical simulation would be too much like their daily work. Remember, the simulation is a deflection technique so it needs to be different. The second important element when choosing an effective simulation is to select one that is based on the same issues targeted in the change effort. There are business simulations that specifically target issues such as teamwork,

> *decision-making, conflict, or interpersonal communication.*
>
> *The business simulation is a deflection technique that is a highly effective way of unfreezing the organization.*
>
> - Steve

Richard Beckhard and David Gliecher's Formula for Change

This is one of only a few OD models that I have seen represented by a formula. Effective Change is a function of:

$$P * FV * FS > R$$

Where:

P represents **Pain** or the level of Organizational Dissatisfaction with the current state

FV represents the **Future Vision** of what is possible

FS represents the **First Steps** (by individual performers) that will make progress towards the future state

R represents **Resistance to change** or what we call the Organizational Immune System™.

In other words, to make effective change, the level of Pain * the Future Vision * clarity about First Steps to achieve the vision all must outweigh the Resistance to change held tight by the Organizational Immune System™.

Organizational **Pain** is the measure of the collective organizational dissatisfaction with the status quo. How much pain is caused in the organization by doing things the way they are now? Are work procedures, policies, or current hierarchy resulting in frustration? Mistrust?

Miscommunication? Low job satisfaction or morale? Or is the current way of doing things tolerable enough to live with?

Beckhard and Gliecher theorized that if people are comfortable with the status quo then the chance for successful change is low. If there is no pain to avoid and no greater pleasure to seek, why would anybody want to ruin a good thing?

Sometimes organizational pain, if not too intense, can become part of the status quo. People learn to live with a low level of pain and are more comfortable with the devil they know than the one they don't. In order to overcome the Organizational Immune System™, the pain level with the status quo can be increased by the Change Champion, who can apply more pressure to the system by doing things like shortening delivery schedules, limiting resources, overloading a bottleneck, or reorganizing a group. These actions can help weaken the barriers to change, but should be used with great caution and only as part of a strategic step in an orchestrated change intervention. Such actions may just move the pain around as people and processes gravitate to the path of least resistance; one person's problem may cause someone else more pain, and the change effort will fail.

Future Vision: When embarking on a change effort, savvy leaders will communicate a high level view of what the future will look like. The Future Vision is not a detailed plan about how to get there; it is only a description of what the future will look like. The Future Vision provides context, direction, alignment, and hope. The change leader must be imbued with this vision and must never tire of communicating it.

> *If the first requirement for change is a sense of dissatisfaction, then the second element in the equation is a vision of what you're going to change to – no engaging vision equals a fear of the unknown. And people will stick with the devil they know rather than the one they don't.*
>
> - Dr. Michael Miles
> Director, Telfer School of Management MBA Program, University of Ottawa
> President, Human Systems Associates Inc.

First Steps: With dissatisfaction of the status quo and a vision of what the future could look like, the next element of successful change is a small series of "baby steps" or specific behaviors that will culminate in the realization of the future vision. The chasm between present state and future state is just too large for individual employees to leap in a single bound. The change leader needs to work with all constituents on the first steps, as this is where the buy-in happens. This is the point at which every performer in the organization can become personally engaged in the change effort. Developing these steps requires careful planning and everyone's involvement. Managers must be ready to loosen the reins, delegate more, and trust the employees. If everyone agrees that they want to escape the pain of the organization as it exists today, and everyone is pointing in the same direction towards the same future goal, and everyone takes one baby step at a time – soon everyone is well on the way to a successful future.

Resistance: The Organizational Immune System™: There are inherent parts of human nature that hold us back from making change. Fear is one of them. Fear of making a mistake, fear of letting go of the predictable past (even if it is somewhat flawed or painful), fear of losing face, loss of status, giving up old procedures that lent power to the holder.

All of these are costs of change that must be overcome. Change leaders must make time to do a lot of hand-holding and reassuring to overcome these things. They must praise the new behaviors, and offer plenty of encouragement along the way. First and foremost they must walk the talk themselves, and demonstrate that they too are making changes in the way they behave. The sentiment that "change is good – you go first" will sink any change effort quicker than an untethered anchor.

Reducing Resistance to Change

There are essentially three ways to reduce resistance in an organization. The first of these is through the provision of information – about the situation, about what others are successfully doing in similar situations, about the possibility that disastrous things will happen unless everyone bands together and does something. The second way to get the ball rolling and reduce resistance along the way is to help people reflect on how the current state contradicts what they believe to be right and virtuous (or even real). This is a values driven strategy of change. It focuses on bringing people face to face with what they believe to be true and showing them that the current situation doesn't live up to that reality or those standards. In psycho-speak this is called cognitive dissonance. People of integrity get hooked by this and so they jump on the change engine. The third strategy is more elementary. It is the power driven strategy. This is where those who have the power simply declare the change as the new reality. If you don't like it, you can leave.

Good change generally involves a judicious mix of all three of these approaches. Often power is used to get things rolling, either with lots of information happening prior to the announcement or, immediately after the announcement. Good Change Champions engage participants in some soul searching too: "Who are we anyway?" or, "Who do you want to be seen as in this industry?" or even, "Where's your pride, man!" Through the discussions

> that follow, the change that was announced and explained becomes a way of achieving that identity or pride. Voilà – the shift has happened.
>
> - Dr. Michael Miles
> Director, Telfer School of Management MBA Program, University of Ottawa
> President, Human Systems Associates Inc.

How This Worked at Mitel

The choice to use Beckhard and Gliecher's model is of particular importance to the Mitel turnaround. The fact that we were trying to shape the behavior of 500 engineers, and the fact that this model is represented as a formula, is no coincidence. This is the model that we strategically selected to teach at the CPL workshops as part of the change management learning. We knew that a change strategy based on a formula would resonate with our engineering audience. We explained to each group that Geoff's mantra of "Quality and Time-To-Market" was his Future Vision, and Kirk's explanation of the company's financial status was his Future Vision. We then tasked each workshop participant to develop a "mini Future Vision" that would be applicable to their particular group, and to work on the First Step behaviors for their group that would get them there. We didn't have to explain that the Tucson Tape, the R&D clock, the pink slip exercise and the slideshow of our decrepit-looking offices were all meant to elevate their level of dissatisfaction with the status quo – they were already there.

We devoted time at each workshop for participants to work on action plans to change processes, procedures, and outmoded rules. Each group would define the First Steps that they would execute upon return to the office. The steps included hunting down Sacred Cows. In taking these First Steps, every person in every group was becoming an owner and a leader of the change process. Geoff reinforced all of this with his elevator chats and positive feedback, and continued lowering the resistance to change. He capitalized on every opportunity to catch people doing right things. When leaders walk the talk, others will walk behind them.

4. Sustainability: Actions and measures that make the gains of change last

Organizational change can be like a large wave crashing onto the shore. It arrives with a lot of energy and noise, but can just as quickly recede and fade to nothing. Making change "stick" is an often-overlooked step in the change process. New behaviors and processes are mostly self-reinforcing and likely to become entrenched over time if they make life easier for employees. Unfortunately, not all new processes or behaviors seem easier or better at the outset and require large amounts of positive reinforcement to keep them going.

It is said that when Spanish conquistador Hernando Cortez landed in Mexico, he ordered his men to burn the ships. Cortez was committed to his mission and wanted to remove the option of going back to Spain. By burning the ships, Cortez and his men were forced to focus on how they could make the mission successful. Sometimes in organizations, the old method needs to be taken away before new behaviors or processes can take hold.

How This Worked at Mitel

Following the CPL workshops, one of our employees developed an intranet website dedicated to Sacred Cows. In short order, we had 72 pages full of Sacred Cows. Employees continued to kill off Sacred Cows and improve things for themselves. Every Sacred Cow killed was like one of Cortez's ships burned. Every time a Sacred Cow got killed, life got easier. We continued the cow theme and used cow mugs, T-shirts and other paraphernalia to reinforce people for killing Sacred Cows, making Quality improvements, or for doing things to ensure that our product release dates were met.

The weekly CDI score reporting process became institutionalized (a process that continues to this day), and we continued to find ways to get the voice of the customer into the development process. We worked with HR to align the performance management and reward systems more closely to achieving our business goals. Sadly, some people could not make the transition to the new culture and left us. However this was oddly reinforcing, as those working hard felt that some laggards had been carried too long.

Our people got a lot of reinforcement from others in the company. R&D was seen as a leading department. The stock price jumped significantly. Once again we were surprised by our transparency, and newspaper articles appeared in the national papers praising the company for being on a roll.

SUMMARY: FRAMEWORK FOR ORGANIZATIONAL CHANGE

1. *People don't resist change, but they do resist being changed.*

    A successful change program creates the right environment to enroll people in making changes happen. Have those who are involved in the change determine the new behaviors needed. Help them to become change agents.

2. *Without the support and commitment of a Change Champion at the organization's senior level, large-scale organizational change is doomed to failure.*

   Enroll senior leaders in the change effort. The best guest speakers and facilitators are well-prepared company leaders. By walking the talk, they can slash resistance to change.

3. *Good diagnostics get past symptoms to root causes of organizational culture.*

   Use this knowledge, combined with a thorough understanding of the company's business goals, to design the required change program. Be alert for the Organizational Immune System™.

4. *A change effort is serious business.*

   Work hard at it. Plan for full-time involvement on the part of the Change Champion and OD professional. Ensure that any workshops consist of a full agenda and that themes are repeated by speakers, simulations, and even any fun exercises. Be prepared to deploy resources to maximize the momentum while the event is still fresh in the minds of all.

5. *A business simulation lowers resistance and builds commitment to the change.*

   Select a simulation as a deflection exercise, and ensure that it presents the same issues as the ailing organization via an unrelated environment.

CHAPTER 18

Some Thoughts On Theory – Dr. Michael Miles

"There's nothing so practical as a good theory."

Kurt Lewin (1951)

THE CHANGE PROGRAM that Steve and Geoff put together at Mitel was critical to the success – in fact, to the survival – of the company. It would have been potentially catastrophic to "just do something", although this approach happens all the time in organizations. This is why the research in change management indicates a 70% failure rate in change projects (and a 78% failure rate in change project in the IT sector.) In planning the Mitel change process, both Steve and Geoff had the wisdom and patience to examine carefully the theoretical underpinnings of potential approaches and to design their program based on those findings, not their gut.

A number of crucial actions that they took stand out to me in retrospect. These actions more or less determined the success of their change, and related clearly to their understanding of various elements of change management theory. Their approach incorporated the following critical actions:

1. They took the time to understand the underlying norms and culture of the organization before they took significant action. In fact, their first "action" was to develop this understanding.

    Prior to the initiation of the change process, I had undertaken a culture review of the Mitel organization as a whole. My interviews indicated that, while there were a variety of dominant themes in the culture, the predominant operational norm was, "Be nice." No ineffective behaviors were confronted in a systematic and determined manner; everyone just turned the other cheek and accepted inappropriate behavior (late deliveries, over-runs on cost, etc.) Such was life at Mitel. The three of us worked together for quite some time to understand precisely what the implications of existing norms were in relation to what was happening, and what needed to happen differently. They also gathered their own data in creative and engaging ways. So, taking time to get legitimate information (Argyris, 1993) to understand the system they were going to change was a very smart move.

2. They understood that their role as change leaders was to *raise the level of dissatisfaction* of key players, not try to make everyone happy. Early on I introduced Steve and Geoff to Beckhard and Gliecher's formula as a framework for thinking through the critical elements of their change process. (They explained this theory well in Chapter 17). In my experience, Steve and Geoff did an exceptionally good job of thinking through their strategies of hooking people into the new – and painful – reality that "things need to be different around here." They used multiple and parallel strategies to achieve

this end. These included:

    a)   *Information.* (The multiple Town Hall sessions and the Tuscon Tapes are excellent examples of this);

    b)   *Deep Experiences* that brought both managers and employees of the R&D Division face to face with the inadequacies of their "business as usual" approach to things. (The integrated business simulation and the Sacred Cows exercises worked exceedingly well here); and

    c)   *Straight Power* (such as when Geoff fired a key manager who clearly was not getting on board.)

3.   Steve and Geoff represented exceptional models of the approach known in the literature as "power with" as opposed to "power over" change management[12]. Each step of the way, their strategy was to figure out how to engage the greatest number of players as possible. The Sacred Cow hunts proved to be a core element of this strategy – and to the success of the change effort. These hunts went on for months and continued to generate positive enthusiasm. The willingness of the change leaders in this case to actively solicit feedback in fun and creative ways energized the whole process. In many respects, they shared control over where the change process took the organization.

The work with Mitel has provided me with innumerable valuable lessons in effective change management practice. I have had the misfortune to work with numerous clients who wanted something "quick and dirty". Working with Steve and Geoff proved very refreshing – and provided experiences that I have shared widely of how to build an effective large system change process in the real world.

Change Assessment Worksheet

Organizational change takes many forms: the implementation of an enterprise-wide computer program, the post-acquisition melding of cultures, and the implementation of significant quality programs such as Six Sigma[13] projects are some examples. Use this worksheet to assess the change readiness of your organization.

Definitions:

Change Champion is the Senior Leadership sponsor who is accountable for the change.

Change Agent(s) is the person or team tasked with day-to-day change activities.

Scoring: Give each answer a 1 if you disagree with the statement, a 5 if you partially agree with the statement, and a 10 if you agree entirely with the statement.

1. LEADERSHIP READINESS

1. Our Change Champion (the most senior person involved in our change effort) is willing and able to devote 100% of her/his time to the change effort, if necessary.
2. Our Change Champion has the organizational power (the title), the financial power (the budget), and the political power (relationship with other organizational powerbrokers) to make this change happen.
3. Our Change Champion has the power to provide all the

necessary resources or training needed to support the change.
4. Our Change Champion leads the part of the organization undergoing the change.
5. Our Senior Leadership team members agree on the business goal(s) that need to change.
6. The business goal(s) that need to change is (are) measurable.
7. Our Senior Leadership team members will support the Change Champion throughout the change process.

2. CURRENT CULTURE ASSESSMENT

8. Our Change Agent has documented the significant events in our company history that have shaped our company culture.
9. Our Change Agent has compiled a comprehensive profile of our existing culture, from all levels, to understand the issues *promoting* this change.
10. Our Change Agent has documented the external factors that are *promoting* this change.
11. Our Change Agent has compiled a comprehensive profile of our culture, from all levels, to understand the issues *restraining* this change.
12. Our Change Agent has analyzed the current undesirable behaviors, and understands the factors that are reinforcing and sustaining them.
13. Our Change Agent has compiled a list of behaviors that must change in order for us to achieve our business goal(s).
14. Our Change Agent and Change Champion are aligned on the list of behaviors that must change in order for us to achieve our business goal(s).

3. INTERVENTION PLAN

15. Our Change Champion consistently communicates a clear, quantifiable definition of what the organization will achieve by making this change.
16. Our Change Champion consistently communicates a clear case for change that answers the question of why we must change.
17. Our Change Agent has designed an event or events to involve employees in the change.
18. Our Change Agent has planned a deflection exercise to reduce the level of resistance to change.
19. We have a scoreboard(s) visible to all employees showing progress towards our business goal(s).
20. A plan is in place to train people on new skills required.
21. All the resources required for employees to be successful are in place.
22. Recognition and reward systems are in place to support those who are changing their behaviors.

4. SUSTAINABILITY ASSESSMENT

23. The employees involved in the change know, and can recite, what is expected of them.
24. The employees involved in the change have the skills to do what is expected of them.
25. The employees involved in the change have the resources to do what is expected of them.
26. The Change Champion and other senior managers personally reinforce those who are making incremental changes.
27. Our People Practices, Performance Management System, and Compensation System have all been adjusted to support and reinforce those who are changing their behavior.

28. Employees are trained in the new way of doing things.
29. The new way of doing things is / will be easier.
30. The old way of doing things is / will be removed.

SCORING:

The assessment above is intended as a checklist to help guide organizations to successful change.

1. LEADERSHIP READINESS

Successful change score: 60 – 70

Some change but it may be in the wrong direction: 45-60

2. CURRENT CULTURE ASSESSMENT

Successful change score: 50 – 70

Some change but it may require a restart: 37 - 50

3. INTERVENTION PLAN

Successful change score: 70 – 80

Some change but it may lack widespread buy-in: 55 - 70

4. SUSTAINABILITY ASSESSMENT

Ideal score = 65 – 80

Some change but it may not last: 50 - 65

CRITICAL PATH SCORES:

The responses to some questions are critical to the success of the change initiative:

A score of less than 10 on questions 2, 11, 13 & 21 will likely lead to failure.

A score of less than 10 on question 26 will likely lead to very slow progress and the possibility of the change being reversed over time.

Footnotes

[1] Mitel was an ISO 9001 Certified Quality Organization. ISO is the International Standards Organization.

[2] Mitel had two divisions: a Semiconductor division and a Systems division. PBX R&D was in the Systems division.

[3] The Organizational Immune System is a Registered Trademark of Sacred Cows Company.

[4] James C. Collins and Jerry I. Porras, *Built to Last: Successful Habits of Visionary Companies* (HarperBusiness 1994).

[5] Ricardo Semler, *Maverick: The Success Story Behind the World's Most Unusual Workplace* (Warner Books, 1993).

[6] Robert Kriegel and David Brandt, *Sacred Cows Make the Best Burgers: Developing Change-Ready People and Organizations* (Warner Books, 1996).

[7] Leslie Wilk Braksick, Ph.D., *Unlock Behavior, Unleash Profit: How Your Leadership Behavior Can Unlock Profitability in Your Organization*, 2nd Edition (The McGraw-Hill Companies, 2007). The **DCOM**® model is a registered trademark of CLG (The Continuous Learning Group Inc.) www.clg.com

[8] Kurt Lewin, *Field Theory in Social Science* (Harper & Row, 1951).

[9] Richard Beckhard, *Organization Development: Strategies and Models* (Addison-Wesley, 1969).

[10] Leslie Wilk Braksick, *Unlock Behavior, Unleash Profits: How Your Leadership Behavior Can Unlock Profitability in Your Organization*, 2nd edition (The McGraw-Hill Companies, 2007).

[11] Quoted from Josep Tura.

[12] Tom Terez, *http:www.betterworkplacenow.com/PowerWith-TomTerez.pdf*, 2007

[13] Developed by Motorola Corporation

Bibliography

Richard Beckhard, Organization Development: Strategies and Models (Addison-Wesley, 1969).

James C. Collins and Jerry I. Porras, *Built to Last: Successful Habits of Visionary Companies* (HarperBusiness 1994).

Robert Kriegel and David Brandt, *Sacred Cows Make the Best Burgers: Developing Change-Ready People and Organizations* (Warner Books, 1996).

Kurt Lewin, *Field Theory in Social Science* (Harper & Row, 1951).

Michael McGrath, *Setting the PACE® in Product Development: A Guide to Product And Cycle-time Excellence* (Butterworth-Heinemann, 1992).

Ricardo Semler, *Maverick: The Success Story Behind the World's Most Unusual Workplace* (Warner Books, 1993).

Leslie Wilk Braksick, Ph.D., *Unlock Behavior, Unleash Profit: How Your Leadership Behavior Can Unlock Profitability in Your Organization*, 2nd Edition (The McGraw-Hill Companies, 2007).

Index

10 questions 58, 60, 61, 62, 135

3-Com 10, 14

A

ABC 149, 157, 168

Antecedent 157

Applied Technical Systems 79

Around here we behave as if (AHWBAI) 37, 89, 165

B

Barons meeting 49, 163

Beckhard, Richard vii, 149, 169, 174, 191, 193

Behavior i, 31, 35, 38, 40, 71, 91, 104, 132, 141, 147, 148, 149, 151, 152, 153, 154, 155, 156, 157, 158, 160, 161, 167, 169, 170, 171, 173, 178, 184, 189

Bell 17

Big Hairy Audacious Goal (BHAG) 71

Body language 37, 62, 132, 152, 153, 154, 160

Boiled Frog Syndrome 166

Braksick Wilk, Leslie vii, 169

Brandt, David 91, 191, 193

British Telecom (B) 9, 12, 45

Built to Last 70, 191, 193

C

Change, Participation and Leadership (CPL) 93

Change Agent i, xi, 24, 31, 47, 53, 67, 75, 85, 111, 119, 127, 132, 140, 151, 187, 188, 189

Change Champion i, xi, 24, 31, 47, 53, 67, 70, 75, 85, 111, 119, 127, 132, 138, 141, 151, 162, 163, 175, 181, 187, 188, 189

Cisco 10, 11, 13, 14

Collins, Gene 60

Collins, James C. 191, 193

Concordia University 88

Consequence 157

Convergence 138

Cowpland, Michael 6

Culture shock 89

Culture treatise 89, 93

Customer Dissatisfaction Index (CDI) 113, 114, 156

D

Dealers 3, 4, 13, 14, 56, 57, 58, 59, 60, 61, 62, 63, 65, 66, 135, 138, 158, 166

Deflection Exercises 88

Demo day viii, 121, 122, 123, 125, 138, 140, 158, 159, 167

Diagnostics 38, 40, 47, 77, 93, 141, 153, 163, 164, 181

Dumont, Ken 59

Duncan, Ian 81

E

Elite Dealers 3, 13, 19, 27, 165

Elite Dealers' Council 3, 13, 19, 27, 165

Engineering 19, 56, 72, 81, 100, 116, 178

Extrovert 72

F

Feature creep 55, 56

Feedback 28, 41, 44, 84, 88, 123, 126, 131, 132, 141, 153, 154, 160, 179, 185

G

Gliecher, David 149, 174

H

Hammer, Michael 64
Human Resources (HR) 6

K

Kanata 5, 34, 36, 57, 58, 61, 135
Kriegel, Robert 91, 191, 193

L

Lannigan, Paul 60
Lennon, Paul 60
Lewin, Kurt vii, 149, 172, 183, 191, 193
Lyon, Steve 60

M

Mandy, Kirk vii, 84, 91, 93, 163
Mate-Link 71
Matthews, Terry 5, 6, 7, 9, 34, 37, 143
Maverick 92, 191, 193
Miles, Michael (Mike) Dr. 15, 17, 18, 140
Millard, John 12, 13, 15, 37, 77, 84, 93
Mitel i, xi, xii, 3, 4, 5, 6, 7, 8, 9, 10, 11, 13, 15, 17, 18, 19, 20, 28, 34, 35, 36, 37, 41, 51, 56, 58, 61, 65, 72, 89, 90, 93, 97, 101, 103, 108, 109, 135, 136, 137, 140, 143, 147, 149, 156, 158, 163, 164, 165, 166, 168, 170, 172, 178, 179, 183, 184, 185, 191

Mitel Networks 143
Munns, Ian 12, 20

N

Near-death experience 9, 14, 166, 167
Newbridge Networks 9
NORMS 154, 155, 160

O

O'Gorman, Chris 141
Organizational Change 24, 53, 151, 179, 187
Organizational development (OD) i, xi, 15, 17, 27, 139, 148, 163
Organizational Immune System 191
Organizational structure 49
Ottawa 5, 15, 18, 176, 178
Outcomes viii, 137

P

Patwell, Beverley vii, 141
Phone 5, 6, 7, 8, 9, 11, 18, 21, 62, 69, 80, 94, 143
Pink slip 92, 101, 105, 136, 167, 178
Private Branch Exchange (PBX) 5
Product management 11, 13, 65, 126
Project management 77, 84
PRTM 43, 78

Q

Quality viii, 15, 18, 19, 21, 22, 25, 27, 38, 55, 58, 69, 70, 72, 73, 74, 78, 101, 109, 113, 114, 115, 116, 117, 126, 130, 133, 135, 138, 156, 158, 159, 163, 166, 167, 170, 178, 180, 191
Quality AND time-to-market 15, 19, 55, 58, 73, 78, 130, 133, 158, 163, 167, 170, 178

R

R&D clock viii, 77, 159
Recognition 189
Research & Development (R&D) i, xi, 3
Resistance to change 174
Rolbin, Sharon 102

S

Sacred cow iv, viii, 87, 91, 94, 100, 104, 106, 108, 109, 110, 133, 134, 136, 140, 156, 160, 179, 180, 185, 113, 116, 121
Sacred Cows Make the Best Burgers 91, 92, 191, 193
Sacred Cow Workshop 100, 104, 108, 109, 113, 133, 134, 136, 140
Semler, Ricardo 91, 191, 193
Sense of urgency 70, 79, 82, 83, 89, 94, 138, 166, 167
Simulations 87, 88, 173, 181
Skills inventory 46
Software 12, 18, 46, 50, 51, 52, 95, 99, 125, 129, 163
Spaghetti syndrome 55, 56
Sustainability 149, 161, 179
SX-200 6, 7, 8, 9, 117
SX-2000 9, 10, 71

T

Technology i, 10, 11, 12, 13, 14, 15
Telco 5, 6, 17
Telephone 4, 5, 10, 11, 64, 69, 101
Time-to-Market viii, 15, 19, 38, 55, 58, 69, 72, 73, 78, 109, 114, 123, 125, 130, 133, 135, 138, 158, 163, 167, 170, 178
Town Hall 36, 37, 71, 72, 73, 81, 82, 115, 116, 122, 133, 185

Tucson Tape viii, 55, 61, 64, 69, 70, 73, 83, 89, 92, 135, 140, 158, 165, 172, 178

U

University of Ottawa 15, 18, 176, 178

V

Voice and data convergence 12
Voice of the customer 56, 58, 60, 65, 66, 67, 104, 138, 166, 180
Voice Over Internet Protocol (VoIP) 12

W

Walking the talk 70, 111, 139, 181

Stephen Quesnelle is an Executive Coach and Behaviorist who has a successful track record of utilizing change management and leadership practices to enhance the performance of organizations in Canada, the U.S., and throughout Europe. Stephen has designed innovative change management and leadership systems to energize and focus employees on activities that add value to their organizations.

Geoff Smith is a Senior Executive who has worked with companies around the globe to help them fulfill their strategic objectives and execute change management programs that led to faster time to market, higher quality and increased profitability. His specific areas of expertise include Leadership and Coaching, Strategic Planning, Customer Relations, Partnerships, Acquisitions and R&D Management.